FRANKENSTEIN

Mary Shelley's Wedding Guest

TWAYNE'S MASTERWORK STUDIES

Robert Lecker, General Editor

FRANKENSTEIN

Mary Shelley's Wedding Guest

Mary Lowe-Evans

TWAYNE PUBLISHERS • NEW YORK
Maxwell Macmillan Canada • Toronto
Maxwell Macmillan International • New York Oxford Singapore Sydney

Twayne's Masterwork Studies No. 126

Frankenstein: Mary Shelley's Wedding Guest
Mary Lowe-Evans

Twayne Publishers
Macmillan Publishing Company
866 Third Avenue
New York, New York 10022

Maxwell Macmillan Canada, Inc.
1200 Eglinton Avenue East
Suite 200
Don Mills, Ontario M3C 3N1

Library of Congress Cataloging-in-Publication Data
Lowe-Evans, Mary.
    Frankenstein: Mary Shelley's wedding guest / Mary Lowe-Evans.
        p.   cm.—(Twayne's masterwork studies; no. 126)
    Includes bibliographical references (p.) and index.
    ISBN 0-8057-8376-8.—ISBN 0-8057-8597-3 (pbk.)
    1. Shelley, Mary Wollstonecraft, 1797-1851. Frankenstein.)
2. Frankenstein (Fictitious character) in literature. 3. Marriage in literature.
4. Monsters in literature. I. Title. II. Series. PR5397.F73L68 1993
823'.7—dc20   92-41553
                                                                    CIP

10 9 8 7 6 5 4 3 2 1 (hc)
10 9 8 7 6 5 4 3 2 1 (pb)

Printed in the United States of America

Contents

"Shelley and Mary in St. Pancras Churchyard." A Victorian conception by W. P. Frith (1819–1909), who sketched the site in the 1870s and modeled the heads on works owned by Sir Percy and Lady Shelley.

Private Collection

Note on the References
and Acknowledgments

Because Penguin Classics are readily available internationally as well as in the United States, and their quality is consistently excellent, I have chosen the 1985 Penguin Classics edition of *Frankenstein*, edited by Maurice Hindle, as my text for this study. Page references to this edition are made parenthetically throughout the work. Like nearly all currently popular editions of *Frankenstein*, the Penguin text follows the third edition of *Frankenstein* (1831), which includes all of Mary Shelley's final revisions and her "Author's Introduction."

The original version of *Frankenstein*, titled *Frankenstein; or, The Modern Prometheus*, was published anonymously in 1818. That version, including an appendix that shows the revisions Mary Shelley made for the 1831 edition, is available in paperback from the University of Chicago Press. While it is important for students to know about this original version, it seems appropriate that they begin their study with the version that is most widely available and discussed and the one that incorporates Mary Shelley's final revisions. Nevertheless, to make students aware of *Frankenstein* as a text-in-progress whose author responded to changes in her culture, I point out, at strategic places in my reading, passages that were added for the 1831 edition.

I would like to acknowledge my mentor and colleague, Patrick A. McCarthy, who encouraged me to begin this work. The cooperation of the University of West Florida's John C. Pace Library staff was

vii

indispensable. In particular, William Lee, Caroline Rowe, and Peggy Toifel helped make my research run smoothly.

My chairman, Philip Momberger, allowed me the time to complete the project on schedule, and his wife, Lynn, did a final reading of the text. My students and my children, Andrea, Stephen, and Stan, have also acted as informed readers.

Finally, my husband and colleague, Ronald V. Evans, provided encouragement, editorial advice, and coffee all along the way.

Preface

The reading of *Frankenstein* that follows takes a biographical-historicist approach to the work. That is, it attempts to clarify certain puzzling issues raised in the novel by relating them to events in Mary Shelley's life and culture. Besides simply clarifying the novel, however, I hope to provide evidence that *Frankenstein* was a living "piece" of early nineteenth-century England and can therefore help us discover how people of that era attempted to resolve their conflicts. How they worked out ethical problems in some sense determined what our ethical problems would be. Therefore, a reading of *Frankenstein* such as this may help students understand our historical legacy so that they may spend it wisely.

With the exception of the final chapter, the focus of the study is what I call the "marriage complex." By this I mean the pervasive interest among early nineteenth-century English men and women in the future of marriage as an institution. There were those, like Mary Shelley's father, William Godwin, and her husband, Percy Shelley, who claimed that the world would be a better place without it. But the majority feared that the dissolution of marriage laws and customs that egalitarianism portended would bring cultural chaos.

More than most young women of her day, Mary Shelley was, through the circumstances of her birth and by her own choice, caught up in controversies about marriage. Her novel *Frankenstein; or, The Modern Prometheus* is very much affected by her involvement in complicated nuptial relationships. Her own eventual marriage and the marriages, near-marriages, and failed marriages of those around her illuminate the essentially conservative themes of the novel. Therefore,

I have devoted most of this study to examining how the characters and events in *Frankenstein* respond and contribute to the debate-in-progress about marriage in the late eighteenth and early nineteenth centuries. So that the reader will not be left uninformed about more traditional ways of interpreting the novel, however, I provide a summary of the romantic and science fiction approaches to *Frankenstein* in the final chapter.

Because a biographical-historicist interpretation requires that the reader have substantial information about Mary Shelley's life and times, I have provided a rather extensive chronology. Chapter 4 also provides extensive biographical information. Both are intentionally slanted toward marital issues, but it should become clear as those issues are examined in context that they were inextricably bound up with other eighteenth- and nineteenth-century cultural reformations.

Chronology: Mary Shelley's Life and Works

1789–1793   Revolution in France, and the Reign of Terror under Robespierre.

1792   Mary Wollstonecraft's *A Vindication of the Rights of Woman* is published.

1793   William Godwin's *An Enquiry Concerning Political Justice* is published.

1794   Fanny Imlay, illegitimate child of Mary Wollstonecraft and the American industrialist Gilbert Imlay, is born 25 August.

1797   Mary Wollstonecraft and William Godwin wed on 29 March at St. Pancras Church, London. Their daughter Mary is born 30 August. Mary Wollstonecraft Godwin dies 10 September from puerperal infection resulting from improper postdelivery medical treatment. Godwin adopts Fanny Imlay.

1798   Wordsworth and Coleridge publish *Lyrical Ballads*, often cited as the beginning of English romanticism. Godwin publishes *Memoirs of the Author of "A Vindication of the Rights of Woman,"* which reveals Mary Wollstonecraft's extramarital affairs (including their own) and her suicide attempts. Godwin is roundly criticized, and Wollstonecraft's influence drastically diminishes for years to come.

1801   Godwin marries Mary Jane Clairmont, whose previous marital history is cloudy. Clairmont brings two children to the marriage, Charles, aged 7, and Jane (later known as Claire), aged 4.

1805   The Godwins open a children's book publishing firm, the Juvenile Library.

1806   Mary hears Coleridge recite *The Rime of the Ancient Mariner*, a work that will considerably influence *Frankenstein*.

1810   The Juvenile Library publishes Mary's first literary work, the poem "Mounseer Nongtonpaw."

1812	Percy Shelley introduces himself to William Godwin in January by way of a letter declaring his ardent admiration of Godwin's *Political Justice*. Percy and his wife Harriet dine with the Godwins in October while Mary is away in Scotland. Mary meets Percy in November.
1813	Shelley's *Queen Mab,* in many respects a poetic revisiting of *Political Justice* but expressing even greater disdain for marriage, is printed and distributed. Paradoxically, Shelley dedicates the poem to his wife.
1814	On 24 March Percy and Harriet Shelley remarry in St. George's Church, London, to establish the legality of their union. Percy and Mary begin seeing one another almost daily; they frequently visit the grave of Mary Wollstonecraft in St. Pancras Churchyard, where they read from her works and biography. Percy and Mary elope to France on 28 July, taking Claire Clairmont along. They continue on to Switzerland, Holland, and Germany, returning to London 13 September. Godwin refuses to see his daughter. Harriet gives birth to Percy's second child, Charles, legal heir to the Shelley estate, on 30 November.
1815	On 22 February Mary gives birth to an illegitimate baby girl, Clara, who dies 6 March. During this period Mary and T. J. Hogg—with Percy's encouragement—carry on an intimate correspondence. Percy invites Harriet to join his household as platonic sister to Mary and himself; Harriet refuses.
1816	An illegitimate son, William, is born to Mary and Percy Shelley on 29 January. Claire Clairmont becomes the mistress of Lord Byron in April. Percy, Mary, William, and Claire join Lord Byron and his physician, John William Polidori, in Switzerland in May. It is the first extended meeting for Shelley and Byron. The group spends several days and nights together in the Villa Diodati at Coligny, where discussions sometime around 15–16 June about "the principle of life" inspire the "waking dream" that will become the central scene of *Frankenstein*. Mary first refers to her "story" (*Frankenstein*) in a 24 July journal entry. Percy, Mary, William, and Claire return to England in September. Fanny Imlay, unable to reconcile herself to her illegitimacy and lack of financial security, commits suicide on 9 October. Harriet Shelley, advanced in pregnancy, the father an unidentified lover, drowns herself in the Serpentine River, where her body is discovered on 10 December. Mary and Percy Shelley marry in St. Mildred's Church, London, on 30 December in a ceremony attended by William Godwin and Mary Jane Clairmont Godwin.

1817	Claire Clairmont gives birth to the illegitimate daughter of Lord Byron, Allegra Alba, on 2 January. Percy is denied legal custody of his and Harriet's two children on 17 March; he apparently never sees them again. Percy, Mary, William, Claire, and Allegra settle together in Albion House in Marlow on 18 May. Mary makes corrections on and transcribes the manuscript of *Frankenstein* during April and apparently completes it in May. After being rejected by two publishers, *Frankenstein* is accepted by Lackington, Hughes, Harding, Mayor & Jones in August. The Shelleys' third child, named Clara after their first one, is born 2 September. Mary's *History of a Six Weeks' Tour,* based on her travels with Shelley, is published in December.
1818	*Frankenstein; or, The Modern Prometheus* is published anonymously in March. The Shelley ménage travels to Italy. Mary begins research for her novel *Valperga* in April. Percy accompanies Claire to Venice to visit Byron. One-year-old Clara dies in September.
1819	Three-year-old William dies of malaria on 7 June. Mary completes an autobiographical novel, *Mathilda,* unpublished in her lifetime. Percy and Mary's only child to survive to adulthood, Percy Florence, is born on 12 November in Florence.
1822	Five-year-old Allegra dies of typhus in April. Mary suffers a miscarriage, which almost costs her her life, on 16 June. Percy Shelley drowns during a storm on 8 July while sailing in the "Don Juan." Mary writes her poem "The Choice."
1823	Sir Timothy Shelley, Percy's father, offers to assume guardianship of Percy Florence in February; Mary refuses. *Valperga* is published. The first dramatic adaptations of *Frankenstein* are performed in London, and the second edition of the novel is published during July and August. Mary and Percy Florence return to England in August. Mary collects and edits *Posthumous Poems of Percy Bysshe Shelley* but is forced to recall the unsold copies at the insistence of Sir Timothy.
1824	Byron dies at Missolonghi, Greece.
1826	Mary's novel *The Last Man* is published in February. Harriet Shelley's son Charles dies in September, making Percy Florence heir to the Shelley estate and title.
1828	Mary writes "The Sisters of Albano" in March, the first of 14 stories to be published in *The Keepsake* between 1828 and 1838. Mary contracts smallpox in April.
1830	Mary's novel *Perkin Warbeck* is published.

1831   A revised edition of *Frankenstein* is published by Bentley and Colburn in their Standard Novels series. It remains the most commonly read and accessible version of the novel to date.

1832   The British Reform Bill, introduced into Parliament the previous year, is enacted, extending the vote to male middle-class businessmen. Woman's suffrage is still more than three-quarters of a century away.

1835   Mary's novel *Lodore* is published, and volumes 1 and 2 of her *Lives of the Most Eminent Literary and Scientific Men of Italy, Spain, and Portugal* are published as part of Lardner's *Cabinet Cyclopedia.*

1836   William Godwin dies on 7 April and is buried with Mary Wollstonecraft in St. Pancras Churchyard. Volume 3 of the *Cabinet Cyclopedia,* Mary's *Lives of the Most Eminent Literary and Scientific Men of Italy, Spain, and Portugal,* is published.

1837   Mary's novel *Falkner* is published.

1838   Volume 1 of Mary's *Eminent . . . Men of France* is published.

1839   Mary's editions of *The Poetical Works of Percy Bysshe Shelley* and *Essays and Letters from Abroad, Translations and Fragments by Percy Bysshe Shelley* are published. Volume 2 of *Eminent . . . Men of France* is published.

1844   Mary's *Rambles in Germany and Italy,* inspired by a trip with Percy Florence and his friends, is published. Sir Timothy dies on 23 April, and Percy Florence succeeds to the Shelley title and inheritance.

1848   Percy Florence marries Jane St. John, an admirer of Mary's who will attempt to "purify" the recorded histories of the Godwins and the Shelleys by insisting that all references to illegitimacy and impropriety in their lives be eliminated.

1851   Mary Shelley dies on 1 February at the age of 53 from a brain tumor. She is buried in St. Peter's Churchyard, Bournemouth, where the transferred remains of her parents rest.

LITERARY AND HISTORICAL CONTEXT

1

Growing Pains

Women's rights, the plight of the laboring class, property distribution, taxation and representation, home artisans versus factory industry, and the educational system (or lack of one) were among the many targets of reform agitation in 1797, the year of Mary Shelley's birth. After being initially sympathetic with the causes of the French Revolution (1789), England had reacted against the extreme measures of the revolutionists and, by 1797, had been at war with France for four years. The arguments pro and con about reform measures would become increasingly strident during the years leading up to the first English Reform Bill in 1832, the year following publication of the final version of *Frankenstein; or, The Modern Prometheus.* It was an age not only of political change but of industrial and scientific transformations throughout the West and of continuing expansion of the British Empire.

The most controversial of these contemporary reform issues inevitably threatened the "inviolable" marriage vow, for energizing all reform movements were the egalitarian philosophies of the American and French revolutions. Carried to its logical conclusion, egalitarianism would give women as well as male laborers and merchants legal, political, and economic parity with men of property, thereby making women independent of marriage contracts for their security and personal dignity. But liberty and equality for all were eventualities as threatening as they were appealing to a majority of the English population in the late eighteenth century.

The egalitarian ideals and chaotic consequences of the French Revolution had simultaneously inspired and horrified the English people. Mary Shelley's father, William Godwin, admitted that his own *Enquiry Concerning Political Justice* (1793) was "a child of the French Revolution,"[1] and Victor Frankenstein's rational, unconventional, but ultimately violent Creature has recently been likened by several critics to that same awe-inspiring event.[2] During the 1780s and 1790s a radical minority group, the so-called English Jacobins—among whom were Mary Shelley's parents—had avidly promoted disestablishment of the aristocracy in favor of individual self-regulation. Securing women's rights was part of their program. In the face of the gratuitous violence and blatant disregard for individual rights in the government of France that followed the Revolution, however, a strong anti-Jacobin movement took hold in England, and William Godwin considerably modified his own anarchical views.

Mary Shelley's milieu was thus characterized by lively controversy over the entire gamut of reform issues, including the reforms that literary romanticism implicitly demanded in its glorification of the individual will, passions, and imagination. Romanticism condoned consciousness-altering experimentation, exalted raw nature, generally distrusted rational trains of thought, and treated ambivalently the considerable advances in science and technology made during the late eighteenth century. Among the numerous influences on the romantic movement, Jean Jacques Rousseau was one of the strongest and most enduring. In his *Discours sur l'origine et les fondements de l'inégalité parmi les hommes* (1755) he compares the innocent, contented man "in a state of nature" with frustrated, restless modern man. Like her parents and husband, Percy Shelley, Mary Shelley avidly read and responded to Rousseau's tenets in her own works. *Frankenstein* provides not only an ironic commentary on the fate of Rousseau's natural man—embodied in the Creature—but, in the character of

Safie, a variation on the theme of women's education (provided by men) that Rousseau sets out in *Julie, ou la Nouvelle Héloïse* (1761).

The alternately exploitive and idealized view of women projected in most romantic literature, including Rousseau's, has been a target of modern feminist criticism, and the dearth of women writers included in the romantic canon is currently the subject of revisionist critiques. But Mary Wollstonecraft's *A Vindication of the Rights of Woman* (1792) and Mary Shelley's *Frankenstein* demonstrate that even in the heyday of Rousseau's literary influence women were disturbed by and writing about the sexist implications of his brand of egalitarianism. Most of the "literature of the imagination," as romantic literature was then known, was produced during the period 1775–1830, the age of Blake, Wordsworth, Coleridge, Keats, Byron, Charles and Mary Lamb, Jane Austen, Percy Shelley, and romanticism's most noted apologist, William Hazlitt. *Frankenstein* was written and revised during the latter half of this period.

Because William Godwin had encouraged his daughter from earliest childhood to use his well-stocked library, she was conversant with virtually all the recognized great works and the more obscure romantic works as well. In fact, because the Godwin home was a veritable salon for the literati, she had met many of the authors. Like other girls, Mary Shelley was educated at home, there being at the time little public support or demand for the institutionalized education of girls, in spite of her own mother's persuasive arguments to the contrary in *The Rights of Woman*.

Mary's reading included popular Gothic novels like Mrs. Radcliffe's *The Mysteries of Udolpho* (1794), M. G. Lewis's *The Monk* (1796), and William Beckford's *Vathek* (1786). *Frankenstein,* however, published in the same year as a heated debate about the moral value of all forms of literature, especially the Gothic novel,[3] is made to stand apart from that 50-year-old form of popular fiction. Cautioning against the power of science (rather than mysterious supernatural forces) to destroy domestic affection and humane inclinations, *Frankenstein* both concludes the Gothic tradition and establishes the science fiction genre. In the preface to the 1818 edition, Percy Shelley (speaking for Mary Shelley in his typically circumlocutious style) avers: "I am by no means indifferent to the manner in which whatever moral tendencies exist in the sentiments or characters it contains shall affect the reader; yet my chief concern in this respect has been limited to the avoiding the enervating effects of the novels of the present day, and to the exhibition of the amiableness of domestic affection, and the excellence of universal virtue" (58). Mary Shelley's reading extended far beyond popular Gothic novels to include such influential political essays of the day as Edmund Burke's *Reflections on the Revolution in France* (1790) and scientific treatises like Humphrey Davy's *Chemical Philosophy* (1812). The influences of all these sources, in complex configurations, can be detected in *Frankenstein,* just as their often contradictory ideologies can be perceived working in the culture at large. The result in *Frankenstein* is a novel whose style and subject stand somewhere between the exotic, egocentric Gothic fiction of the eighteenth century and the community-minded social novels of the Victorian era.

Besides the egalitarianism promised by the American and French revolutions, many of the English at the turn of the century were also seduced by scientific advancements and the early successes of an expanding empire. In 1812 Britain was once again at war with the United States, while the wars with Napoleon's France continued. Meanwhile, there was a growing faith among scientists like Humphrey Davy that science could transcend national differences and provide answers to the mysteries of life and human suffering. Evangelicalism, a return to the fundamentals of Christianity and in many ways a reaction against this faith in science, made significant inroads in traditional religious institutions, including the Anglican church. On the other hand, *Frankenstein,* also a warning about obsessive glorification of science, seems to leave religion out of the cultural picture altogether, even as it assigns typically theological terms to the activity of Victor Frankenstein, the "creator." The influence of William Godwin and Percy Shelley, both avowed atheists convinced of humankind's natural good nature, might be detected in *Frankenstein's* implicit argument that natural goodness is susceptible to perversion by institutionalized disciplines like science.

Travel abroad and—for those who could not afford such luxury—reading travel books had become popular pastimes by 1800. Romanticizing faraway places not only titillated pedestrian imaginations, as Gothic novels did, but encouraged continued expansion of the empire. Mary Shelley's *History of a Six Weeks' Tour* (1817), taken from the memoirs of her first hectic trip to the Continent with Percy Shelley and Claire Clairmont, contributed to the growing number of such guides. Many of the detailed descriptions of nature in *Frankenstein* exhibit a romantic reverence for nature and subtle dissatisfaction with the tame landscapes of home that anticipate the style and attitude of her travelogue.

At the conclusion of the Napoleonic Wars in 1815, England had greatly increased its territorial possessions and international political power; the desire to expand had thus been very briefly satiated. At home, however, England was burdened with overwhelming debt and a recently formed working class that feared being replaced by ever newer technologies. The Luddites exemplify one group of disgruntled skilled workers. Framework knitters of gentlemen's stockings, their positions became threatened by new machinery that produced stockings more cheaply. Despite aggressive protests not only about their economic plight, but also about the insult to their skill and dignity, the Luddites were forced to give way to advanced technology. Also during this period, hundreds of disgruntled, out-of-work soldiers and sailors were deposited in the seaport towns of England by returning warships. A population increasing at an alarming rate coupled with several years of massive crop failures added to domestic discontents, and the movement of farmhands into the overcrowded cities exacerbated the situation. Rioting had become frequent and violent. While the slave trade was abolished throughout the British Empire in 1816, the Irish were beginning to agitate for independence.

The economic squeeze characteristically affecting the middle and lower classes during these years dramatically affected Mary Shelley's family as well. Mrs. Godwin's Juvenile Library had failed and Godwin was irregularly engaged in writing. Never a practical man, William Godwin had been incapable of adjusting to the diminished financial resources his fall from public grace had brought. Furthermore, he had not been emotionally prepared to direct the activities of the large family he had acquired almost by default. Eventually, Godwin would turn to Percy Shelley for financial assistance, even during the years when he estranged himself from Mary for eloping with the young poet.

Both William Godwin's and Percy Shelley's attitudes toward economic egalitarianism were influenced by the philosophy of Jeremy Bentham. Known as "the father of utilitarianism," Bentham argued for "the greatest happiness of the greatest number," and his principles were widely argued by liberal politicians and the working classes alike. Not surprisingly, utilitarianism was distorted to fit capitalism's laissez-faire philosophy. It was out of this cultural broil, where utilitarianism bred with romanticism, evangelicals challenged High Church elitists, pride of empire was deflated by domestic unrest, and the propertied aristocracy came under attack from the increasingly more educated but economically disenfranchised masses, that *Frankenstein* emerged.

2

A Perennially Modern Myth

From roughly 1850 until the 1960s, *Frankenstein* might have seemed important only as the original inspiration of such wildly diverse cinematic variants as *The Bride of Frankenstein* (1935), *Abbott and Costello Meet Frankenstein* (1948), and *Young Frankenstein* (1975). Such hideous progeny still proliferate. *The Rocky Horror Picture Show* (1975), one of the most bizarre film variations, has acquired a cult following. And the 1990 soft-porn film *Frankenhooker* is quickly gaining fans. Until recently, however, anyone who knew anything about pop culture in the Western world knew the bare plot of *Frankenstein* without ever having read the novel. It was rarely included in courses of study or even mentioned in texts purporting to introduce the romantic period. On the other hand, it has never gone out of print.

In the 1970s the importance of *Frankenstein* as something more than an engaging horror story began to be widely recognized. That recognition is directly attributable to the rise of interest in women's studies and the establishment of science fiction as a genre respectable enough to be studied in universities. Currently, *Frankenstein* may be found on the syllabuses of courses in romanticism, women writers, science fiction, young adult literature, and ethics.

The range of courses in which *Frankenstein* is taught implies the reasons for its importance. As both critique and exemplar of romantic tenets, *Frankenstein* is without equal. The themes of isolation, the consolation provided by sublime nature, the power of the imagination, and the Promethean power and limitations of man are all explored. But each theme interacts with every other so that the novel's message can never be reduced to the simple terms to which many poetical works of the romantic period reduce these themes. In effect, *Frankenstein* demonstrates that the romantic response to the rationality of the Enlightenment is as fraught with danger to the human community as were Enlightenment doctrines themselves. Mary Shelley's work represents the complexity of familiar romantic themes not only through the language of the novel but in its structure and situations. The narrative within a narrative within a narrative underscores the difficulty of ever getting at the truth of things as they really are or were. The epistolary form further draws attention to the selectivity—and therefore the limited nature—of our knowledge. On the other hand, the novel's multiple points of view suggest that no *single* narrator is reliable, but the *community* of narrators may approach something like truth.

As an extraordinarily influential critique of Western culture written by a woman, *Frankenstein* has recently received intense scrutiny. The contributions of female characters to the major arguments of the novel offer rich grounds for analysis. But here again, Mary Shelley does not oversimplify. The feminine *role* in *Frankenstein* is actually dispersed into a composite including all females, from the absent Margaret Saville and the ill-fated female Creature to Elizabeth Lavenza, Justine, and Safie. Only recently has the significance of these characters and their positioning in the novel been noted. Feminist critics have demonstrated the astute cultural critique offered not only in descriptions of these women but in where and how they enter the various narratives. The emphasis on a feminine perspective, furthermore, often leads out of the text of *Frankenstein* and into the lives of Mary Shelley and her mother, Mary Wollstonecraft. Since Mary Wollstonecraft produced one of the landmark works of feminist writing, and her influence on

Frankenstein's author is considerable, the novel itself becomes important as a stimulus for serious study of an entire critical movement that continues to challenge genderized roles.

While courses in women's studies may recognize *Frankenstein* as one of many feminist critiques of patriarchal attitudes and behaviors, most science fiction courses honor *Frankenstein* as the original of the genre. Because it demonstrates the uses of a "false front of scientific thinking as a disguise within which unscientific motives . . . drive the plot,"[1] *Frankenstein* neatly fits into the category it originated. But recently critics have come to appreciate that *Frankenstein*'s depiction of the state of contemporary science was not altogether false. In fact, *Frankenstein* directly challenges a number of once and future scientific theories so as to highlight their ethical complexity. For example, nineteenth-century biological theory aimed at manipulating evolutionary processes (as represented by Erasmus Darwin, Charles Darwin's grandfather) is a special target for criticism in *Frankenstein*. But recent experimentation with genetic engineering makes the implicit warnings of *Frankenstein* also decidedly modern. Moreover, the likelihood that scientific experimentation and technological "advances" will continue to be made without serious regard for their ethical consequences seems to ensure the eternal timeliness of *Frankenstein* and its place as the quintessential work of science fiction.

The widening focus of literary criticism from the isolated text to the work in contexts—for instance, biographical, historical, psychological, ideological—has brought to attention *Frankenstein*'s value as both an impressive first novel by an adolescent author and a complex treatment of cultural ethics. That Mary Shelley began writing *Frankenstein* when she was just 18 and published it when she was 20 is incredible in any era, for the variety and effectiveness of the novel's literary, political, and scientific allusions alone render it a sophisticated treatment of chronic moral problems. Additionally, the narrative structure, the number, variety, and relationships of the characters, even the novel's circumlocutions underscore the controlling theme—the interrelatedness of all human activity. For example, Victor Frankenstein's carefully established roles—son, fiancé, student, mentor, friend, and "parent"—all draw attention to his failed relationships with others and also to the vexed relationship between the romantic vision and reality.

Young readers who learn something of Mary Shelley's life seem more willing to seriously critique her book and the cultural milieu that helped produce it. Among Mary Shelley's frustrations during the period of *Frankenstein*'s composition were the unexpected alienation from her beloved father, the death of her prematurely born daughter, and her growing antagonism toward her ever-present stepsister, Claire Clairmont. Besides being the work of an author with whom young readers can sympathize, *Frankenstein* is a work that mature scholars in the recent past also take most seriously. Thus, *Frankenstein* is valuable as a catalyst for communication about values across generations.

Finally, as several critical studies and the continuing proliferation of literary and film variants of the novel demonstrate, *Frankenstein* is valuable because it is a perennially modern myth. It not only verbalizes some of our culture's deepest and most persistent fears but demonstrates the disastrous consequences when a scientist-hero ignores responsibility to the community. Thus, like all true myths, it attempts to establish a pattern of moral behavior that is acceptable and beneficial to the culture. *Frankenstein* has endured, reproduced itself, and yet remains young; it is a literary artifact eminently worth investigating.

3

Critical Reception

Percy Shelley wrote the preface to the original three-volume edition of
Frankenstein, and Mary Shelley dedicated it to "William
Godwin/Author of *Political Justice, Caleb Williams,* etc." It is not surprising, then, that the earliest critics reviewed *Frankenstein* in terms of
its relationship to Godwin and his most famous disciple, Percy Shelley.
The reviews were numerous and somewhat mixed but generally favorable, and from all accounts the novel was enthusiastically received by
the reading public of 1818. Even the women's magazine *La Belle
Assemblée* reviewed it favorably without knowing its author was a
woman. The conservative *Quarterly Review* observed with some distaste that "dedicated to Mr. Godwin [it was] written in the spirit of his
school. . . . It inculcates no lesson of conduct, manners or morality; it
cannot mend, and will not even amuse its readers unless their taste
have been deplorably vitiated."[1] The mixture of popular praise and
mixed "literary" response has marked the critical history of
Frankenstein almost to the present day.

    After receiving a copy of the novel from Percy Shelley, Sir Walter
Scott produced in 1818 an eight-page review for the liberal
Blackwood's Edinburgh Magazine praising the novel. Believing that

Shelley had actually written it, Scott held that, "formed in the Godwinian Manner [the novel] has all the faults but likewise the beauties of that model." He extolled the clarity and force of the language, observing that "his descriptions of landscape have in them the choice requisites of truth, freshness, precision, and beauty."[2] Ironically, critics would later discover that the fresh, clear language was Mary Shelley's own, while much of the circumlocutionary "dead wood" was added by Percy Shelley in his role as editor.[3] Like many a critic after him, Scott questioned certain improbabilities in the novel, especially regarding the Creature's education and undetected crimes; but on balance he saw fit to "congratulate our readers upon a novel which excites new reflections and untried sources of emotion" (Scott, 253).

Perhaps the reviews most important to Mary Shelley were those of her husband and her father. Percy Shelley's favorable review, unpublished until after his death, asserted among other things that "the direct moral of the book consists [in:] Treat a person ill, and he will become wicked."[4] William Godwin was delighted with his daughter's accomplishment, proclaiming the novel "the most wonderful work to have been written at twenty years of age that I have ever heard of." But he was off the mark when he predicted that *Frankenstein* was "too good ever to be popular" (St. Clair, 438). Subsequent critics up until the recent past were less enthusiastic than Godwin about the literary quality of the novel, but few have denied its power. William Beckford, author of *Vathek,* recorded his informal critique on the flyleaf of his own copy of *Frankenstein:* he condemned it as "perhaps, the foulest toadstool that has yet sprung up, from the reeking dunghill of the present times."[5] Beckford seems to have been more offended by Mary Shelley's unadorned style of writing, however, than by the novel's subject matter. Even Percy Shelley's interpolations did not force *Frankenstein* into the florid style Beckford appears to have required.

To capitalize on an early version of the novel, *Presumption; or, The Fate of Frankenstein* (one of hundreds of dramatic transformations to follow), William Godwin arranged to have *Frankenstein* reissued in two volumes in 1823. But it was not until 1831 that the single-volume edition most commonly read today was published. Revised and introduced by Mary Shelley herself, the 1831 edition of *Frankenstein* is more conservative than the original, especially with regard to women's roles, for it adheres more closely to the popular notion that men and women naturally function in complementary but separate spheres of influence. Furthermore, Mary Shelley's revisions align the 1831 *Frankenstein* more closely with conventional marriage customs than had the original. For example, Elizabeth, Victor's blood relative in the 1818 edition, becomes a foundling in 1831, and the senior Frankensteins' marriage becomes more idealized. Since its publication, Mary Shelley's apologetic "Author's Introduction," which briefly describes the circumstances of the rainy hiatus at the Villa Diodati where *Frankenstein* was conceived, has become inseparable from the text of *Frankenstein* and, like the novel itself, has been variously interpreted. Even the accuracy of the Villa Diodati account has been questioned. Surprisingly, Henry Crabb Robinson, one of the few reviewers who read *Frankenstein* for the first time in 1831, found it "disgusting" and—perhaps to mitigate that disgust—felt that it should have been set in medieval rather than modern times.[6]

Until the 1960s critics generally paid more attention to Percy Shelley's influence on *Frankenstein* than to Mary Shelley's accomplishment. An exception is M. A. Goldberg's 1959 article "Moral and Myth in Mrs. Shelley's *Frankenstein*."[7] Goldberg relocates the novel in its social context to show how it responded to the cultural call for moral guidance in the early 1800s. By focusing on both text *and* context, Goldberg anticipates the current tendency in *Frankenstein* criticism to attempt to account for the novel's popular as well as its literary appeal. In spite of Goldberg's analysis and other favorable critical views of the novel, in the 1964 entry in *Masterplots,* the only critique that most students of the novel would read in the decade of 1965–75, the unnamed critic finds *Frankenstein* "a wholly incredible story told with little skill." Adding insult to injury, he contends that "Mary Shelley would be remembered if she had written nothing, for she was the wife of Percy Bysshe Shelley under romantic and scandalous circumstances."[8] Fortunately, Harold Bloom's 1965 interpretation, "*Frankenstein;* or, The New Prometheus," takes Mary Shelley's work more seriously, treating it as a counterargument to Promethean romanticism.[9] Since then,

Frankenstein has been recognized as the ingenious, complex creation of a young woman who registered and questioned myriad influences in her cultural milieu. Some of the most innovative modern readings of *Frankenstein* have come from women critics; Ellen Moers, for example, is credited with breaking the ground for subsequent feminist interpretations. During the past 20 years, critical studies of the novel have become as numerous, and in some cases as bizarre, as the film variants. One of the first to recognize the number and variety of influences on *Frankenstein* was Christopher Small whose *Ariel Like a Harpy* (1954) demonstrates Mary Shelley's complex use of romantic themes, as does L. J. Swingle's "Frankenstein's Monster and Its Romantic Relatives: Problems of Knowledge in English Romanticism" (1973).[10]

The 1979 collection of essays *The Endurance of "Frankenstein"* is the capstone of the first decade during which the novel received serious attention from a wide range of critics. This collection of primarily scientific and popular-culture readings also includes Ellen Moers's seminal essay, "Female Gothic," which focuses on *Frankenstein*'s treatment of birth-as-death.[11] Sandra Gilbert and Susan Gubar discuss *Frankenstein* in their 1979 benchmark feminist treatise of women's writing, *The Madwoman in the Attic;* they interpret it as a revisiting of *Paradise Lost.*[12] These two feminist pieces anticipate the embarrassment of riches to come in feminist critiques of *Frankenstein* in the 1980s and 1990s.

Barbara Johnson's "My Monster/My Self" (1982) discusses *Frankenstein*'s concerns with the woman writer, mothering, and autobiography.[13] Mary Poovey treats Mary Shelley as part of a continuum of women writers in *The Proper Lady and the Woman Writer* (1984).[14] Poovey, as much a cultural critic as a feminist, considers *Frankenstein* in relation to the plethora of conduct manuals for women written in the late eighteenth and early nineteenth centuries. Gayatri Spivak locates the novel in an even larger cultural context, that of British imperialism, in "Three Women's Texts and a Critique of Imperialism" (1985).[15] In *Mary Shelley and "Frankenstein": The Fate of Androgyny* (1986), William Veeder makes a strong case for *Frankenstein*'s place in what he sees as Mary Shelley's ongoing argument in favor of an androgynous cultural vision.[16] Anne Mellor's *Mary Shelley* (1988) places *Frankenstein* solidly in the context of Mary Shelley's conflict-ridden life and times, expanding upon the basic biographical information provided in such works as William Walling's *Mary Shelley* (1972), Jane Dunn's *Moon in Eclipse: A Life of Mary Shelley* (1978), and Muriel Spark's revision of her earlier work, *Child of Light: A Reassessment of Mary Wollstonecraft Shelley* (1951).[17] Mellor's work also provides valuable textual-historicist criticism: she shows how the changes in the 1831 text of *Frankenstein* alter the vision of the original 1818 version. Amid the numerous feminist and gender-focused readings of *Frankenstein* published during the 1980s, Chris Baldick's *In Frankenstein's Shadow* (1987) offers valuable insights about the transformations and usurpations of *Frankenstein* by other genres (even political cartoons) and by (mostly male) authors, such as Joseph Conrad.

Alongside cultural and feminist critiques of the novel, psychoanalytical and science fiction readings have proliferated and have tended to incorporate feminist issues. Rosemary Jackson's "Narcissism and Beyond: A Psychoanalytic Reading of *Frankenstein* and Fantasies of the Double" (1986) and Judith A. Spector's "Science Fiction and the Sex War: A Womb of One's Own" (1981) are cases in point.[18] Samuel Holmes Vasbinder in "Scientific Attitudes in Mary Shelley's *Frankenstein*" (1984) and Theodore Ziolkowski in "Science, Frankenstein, and Myth" (1981) both focus more exclusively on issues of science in the novel.[19] Complementing such readings, which rely on extratextual information, Henriette Lazaridis Power's "The Text as Trap: The Problem of Difference in Mary Shelley's *Frankenstein*" (1988) epitomizes a type of deconstructive reading that focuses on the framed narratives within the text.[20]

In assessing the novel's critical heritage, Donald Glut's *The Frankenstein Catalog* (1984), an annotated bibliography of *Frankenstein* variants, editions, and critiques, is instructive.[21] By bringing together descriptions of *Frankenstein*'s hundreds of descendants, it establishes the tremendous suggestive power of the work, and by listing and annotating virtually all extant works about *Frankenstein,* it makes clear the type and degree of scholarly attention the novel has inspired throughout its history. All told, there are 2,666 entries in

Glut's list, ranging from translations to sheet music. Nonetheless, *The Frankenstein Catalog* needs a considerable update since its publication less than a decade ago. A recent example of *Frankenstein*'s progeny, and a tribute to its hold on the popular imagination, is the collection of stories *The Ultimate Frankenstein* (1991), compiled in honor of the sixtieth anniversary of the Boris Karloff film and introduced by Isaac Asimov.[22]

The almost simultaneous publication of the Modern Language Association's *Approaches to Teaching Frankenstein* (1990) and the St. Martin's "Critical Casebook" edition (1992) attests to the growing institutional popularity of the novel. *Approaches,* aimed specifically at teachers, is a sourcebook that includes feminist, science fiction, psychoanalytical, and romantic essays on *Frankenstein,* as well as lists of reference works, editions of the novel, and suggested contexts of study.[23] The Critical Casebook edition, directed at college students, includes the "Complete, Authoritative Text with Biographical and Historical Contexts, Critical History, and Essays from Five Contemporary Critical Perspectives," including those of reader response, psychoanalytical, feminist, Marxist, and cultural criticism.[24]

What is clear in the recent critical history of *Frankenstein* is that there is no longer much question of its "literary" value. The boundaries and conventions of literature have been challenged in recent years so that previously neglected works and genres are being reassessed and works that have maintained a place in popular culture, like *Frankenstein,* are being given the attention their tenacity demands. Modern critiques of the novel tend to draw on numerous schools of criticism, especially feminist, psychoanalytical, cultural, and biographical. The most satisfying are those that recognize the richness of *Frankenstein* and its resistance to any single approach. Ironically, the serious attention the novel is currently receiving from the academic community will very likely ensure its place in the "canon" of literary masterpieces at a time when the very existence of that honored corpus is under attack by feminist and other poststructuralist critics.

A READING

4

Wedding Guests—Wedding Ghosts

> I could not so easily get rid of my hideous phantom; still it haunted
> me.
>
> —"Author's Introduction" (55)

In her introduction to the 1831 edition of *Frankenstein*, Mary Shelley recalls Lord Byron having inspired her tale about "the pale student of unhallowed arts" with a challenge: "We will each write a ghost story" (55, 53). But *Frankenstein* turned out to be much more than a conventional hair-raiser. Over a period of 15 years Mary Shelley shaped it into a multidimensional cautionary tale about the consequences of various excesses and imbalances in society. Though Victor Frankenstein and his Creature appear at first to be responsible for all the violence and anguish in the novel, a closer look reveals that each character, as well as the conventions of society, must share blame for the victims' deaths and even for Victor's downfall. Through multiple frames—each added after Mary Shelley conceived the original scene of the monster's creation, each providing a retrospective view of Victor's tragedy— numerous "ghosts" *do* come into view, including ghosts from Mary

Shelley's own past; these haunting memories pervade the novel. Two of the most influential spirits that inhabit the text of *Frankenstein* are Mary Shelley's mother and father.

In spite of their frequent public criticisms of institutionalized marriage, her parents wed at St. Pancras Church, London, on 29 March 1797, five months before Mary was born. They did so to spare Mary Wollstonecraft the kind of ostracism she had experienced when she had borne Gilbert Imlay's child out of wedlock three years earlier. The inherent contradictions in the tardy but conventional ceremony uniting Mary Wollstonecraft and William Godwin, two notorious radicals, might be taken as a sign of the seriously vexed attitude about marriage and legitimacy that marks Mary Shelley's "hideous progeny" (56). *Frankenstein* registers her approach-avoidance response to the institution of marriage, the roles it seemed to demand of husband and wife, the security it ostensibly provided, and the psychological stress it inevitably involved.

Recently feminist critics have explored a variety of issues *Frankenstein* raises about women's roles, psychology, education, and expectations. Anne Mellor treats *Frankenstein* as a sign of Mary Shelley's frustrated desire for an ideal domestic circle where parental roles would be balanced and children of both sexes valued, loved, and intellectually challenged. My reading owes much to Mellor's insights, and in the main concurs with them. However, my emphasis is different. I hope to reveal that *Frankenstein* is as much an indictment of institutionalized marriage—with its foundation in the "separate-sphere" philosophy—as a lament over failed relationships or Promethean arrogance. But the caveat to would-be marriage partners that *Frankenstein* offers is both subtle and tentative, partly because Mary Shelley was not altogether sure how she felt about marriage herself, and partly because she modified the 1831 version of *Frankenstein* under cultural pressure to establish marriage as the moral fixative of society.

The wedding guest-ghost conundrum of this chapter's title refers not only to Mary Shelley being haunted by her parents and their complicated marriage philosophies and behaviors, but to the fact that her mother died ten days after Mary's birth, thus literally becoming Mary's ghostly inspiration. Her beloved father remarried four years later. This second marriage of William Godwin—an avowed antimatrimonialist—imposed on Mary a stepmother she resented and a stepsister she alternately admired and despised.

Percy Shelley also provided Mary with an utterly inconsistent model of matrimonial behavior, and his spirit animates Victor Frankenstein, who was, like Percy Shelley and William Godwin, a reluctant bridegroom. Though heir-apparent to an aristocratic title and fortune, Percy Shelley advocated the lawless, egalitarian marriage philosophy William Godwin had espoused in his youth. Nonetheless, when he met and fell in love with Godwin's bright, accomplished daughter, he was already a married man with one child and another on the way. Just before Percy Shelley eloped with Mary, he *re*married his first wife, Harriet, to ensure the legal rights of his two children. Only Harriet Shelley's tragic suicide—which took place in the early stages of *Frankenstein*'s composition—made it possible for Mary Godwin to become Mrs. Percy Shelley and for her children to become legitimate. Years later, in a 12 February 1839 journal entry, Mary Shelley was to remember the ghost of "poor Harriet, to whose sad fate I attribute so many of my own heavy sorrows, as the atonement claimed by fate for her death."[1] But when Harriet's death was discovered, Mary seems to have suppressed her emotions and wasted no time legitimizing her union with Percy Shelley.

Throughout *Frankenstein* marital and parent-child relationships are highlighted, examined, and evaluated. The relationships are varied and complex, making it difficult to decide just how Mary Shelley's ghosts influence the novel. But Elizabeth's wedding-night murder, and the destruction of the female monster to prevent her union with the Creature, strongly suggest that entry into marriage was a troublesome passage for Mary Shelley. What's more, the termination of these two characters projects a hopelessness about the future of egalitarian marriage generally that is difficult to deny and only slightly offset by the apparently happy marriages scattered throughout the novel.

In succeeding chapters I will focus on controversial issues involving marriage and legitimacy that intrude on the story of Victor Frankenstein and his Creature. For the remainder of this chapter, I hope to show *how* the marriage complex provides an effective key to understanding a work ostensibly written to caution readers against obsessive devotion to science and exploration.

As Mary Shelley originally conceived it, *Frankenstein* was to begin with the opening scene of chapter 5: "It was on a dreary night of November that I beheld the accomplishment of my toils" (101). The idea of the overweening scientist creating in isolation a being he cannot control is therefore the seed of the novel; in fact, the scene of creation is the focus of most film versions. Unlike the film version, however, the novel immediately juxtaposes Victor's horror at the scientific deformation he has created with a wild dream about his fiancée: "I thought I saw Elizabeth, in the bloom of health, walking in the streets of Ingolstadt. . . . As I imprinted the first kiss on her lips, they became livid with the hue of death; her features appeared to change, and I thought that I held the corpse of my dead mother in my arms" (102). Even here in the original "workshop of filthy creation" (98), Mary Shelley emphasizes that Victor Frankenstein's sin is in some sense an anticonjugal one. He is immediately tortured by a sense of having endangered his future spouse, and indeed the dream foreshadows Elizabeth's death at the hands of the Creature. But his unconscious also senses that this act of his is a betrayal of his dead mother, whose "firmest hopes of future happiness were placed on the prospect of [Victor and Elizabeth's] union" (87). Coming directly on the heels of the Creature's animation, the dream implies that Victor's sin is a sin against his vow to Elizabeth as well as a sin of presumption.

As the story of Victor Frankenstein's ruin took shape in her mind, Mary Shelley added layers and frames to the original scene of creation that would make the novel sensitive to the problems surrounding "domestic affection" (58), as Percy Shelley called it in his preface to the 1818 edition. She moved her story out of Victor Frankenstein's attic laboratory in Ingolstadt and into his home in Geneva, and into his past, to show how the sin of the Promethean scientist was both caused by and damaging to domestic affiliations. Nor did she stop with Victor's home. Adding a framework of letters written to a married woman in England who is in many respects like herself, she connected Victor's crime with her own personal world of domestic affections. Also, by allowing Percy Shelley "carte blanche to make what alterations [he] please[d],"[2] she made him a sort of ghost-writer of her novel and rendered it a product of their union. Finally, by placing Robert Walton aboard a ship headed for the Arctic Circle and sending Victor Frankenstein to Scotland and Ireland on a futile mission to undo his crime, she expanded her cautionary tale out of the domestic circle to include the British Empire.

In the very first of the letters that frame *Frankenstein,* Robert Walton speaks of domestic conflicts, especially strictures that family relationships have placed on him: "My father's dying injunction had forbidden my uncle to allow me to embark on a seafaring life" (60). Only an unexpected inheritance allows Walton to ignore his father's injunction and act on his aspirations. In the second letter Walton returns to the subject of patriarchal power, recounting the story of a father who "would never consent to the union" (65) of his daughter with an impoverished young man. From these seemingly inconsequential references to the law of the father within and over the institution of marriage, the narrative moves into a veritable labyrinth of marital histories, ranging from that of Victor Frankenstein's grandparents to the imagined results of the Creature's union with a female of his species: "A race of devils would be propagated upon the earth who might make the very existence of the species of man a condition precarious and full of terror" (206).

Many of the conflicts troubling Mary Shelley herself in 1816 might be read into these puzzling references. She was deeply affected by her father's rejection as a result of her elopement with Percy Shelley. Meanwhile, Shelley suffered financially and emotionally from the refusal of both his father and grandfather to finance his various enterprises; his stress was always shared by Mary. Mary also suffered physically from the repeated pregnancies and miscarriages her union with Shelley incurred. Psychologically she was troubled during the novel's early development knowing that, because she could not marry Percy Shelley, she and her offspring were illegitimate. They were therefore liable to be objects of discrimination and cultural ostracism, as her mother and her half-sister, Fanny Imlay, had been. Like Victor

Frankenstein's Creature, they would be legally handicapped, if not "monsters."

Mary Shelley's private stress was typical of the more public cultural unease about marriage. The various marriage relationships in the novel represent an attempt to work out or write out not only Mary Shelley's but also her culture's discontents with the inequities implicit in the marriage bond. Thirteen years after *Frankenstein*'s original publication, a period during which not only a plethora of texts argued the need for strong marriages but Mary Shelley herself felt pressure to support her family through her writing, she composed her "Author's Introduction" to *Frankenstein*. Ostensibly meant to "account for the origin" of her strange story (51), this introduction reveals her unremitting and increasing concern about the position of the individual within the institution of marriage.

One might argue that the introduction provides the novel another narrative frame in addition to the Robert Walton letters and the story within a story she had established earlier. In the second paragraph she calls attention to her parentage: "It is not singular that, as the daughter of two persons of distinguished literary celebrity, I should very early in life have thought of writing" (51). Thus, this final, outside frame around the central scene of *Frankenstein* provides an entry into her biography and seems to suggest that Mary Shelley's own real-life parents must share some of the responsibility for the "dreary night of November" when a horrified Victor Frankenstein "beheld the accomplishment of [his] toils."

Continuing to account for the origin of *Frankenstein,* she credits Lord Byron and the influence of "my husband," who she insists "was from the very first anxious that I should prove myself worthy of my parentage and enrol myself on the page of fame" (52). These two imposing literary figures, both dead by the time she wrote the introduction, haunted her life and works as tenaciously as her parents. That Mary Shelley refers to Percy Shelley here as her "husband" is both revealing and deceptive. At the point in the prehistory of *Frankenstein* to which she refers he was decidedly *not* her husband, but the husband of another woman. Yet Mary Shelley chose to include references to him as her spouse that might just as easily have been left out. Looking back on the early illegitimate relationship, which caused both her and Shelley such anguish and could have caused her great embarrassment even in 1831, she decided to legitimize it.

Going on to describe *Frankenstein*'s development, she adopts a tone about Percy Shelley that might easily be interpreted as resentful:

> He was forever inciting me to obtain literary reputation, which even on my part I cared for then, though since I have become infinitely indifferent to it. At this time he desired that I should write, not so much with the idea that I could produce any thing worthy of notice, but that he might himself judge how far I possessed the promise of better things hereafter. Still I did nothing. Travelling, and the cares of a family, occupied my time; and study, in the way of reading or improving my ideas in communication with his far more cultivated mind, was all of literary employment that engaged my attention. (52)

In this passage Mary Shelley both undervalues her own talent in favor of her husband's and disclaims any current ambitions for "literary reputation." That disclaimer, and her mention of "the cares of a family," incorporate the conventional, conservative attitude that a proper, middle-class, married Englishwoman in 1831 was expected to take. That attitude is grounded in the separate-sphere philosophy, which I will discuss at greater length in chapter 5. Suffice it to say here that "literary reputation," even for the "daughter of two persons of distinguished literary celebrity," came at an extraordinarily high price. For a woman of public reputation must clearly be neglecting the more important job of caring for the family.

In fact, Mary Shelley cared very much for her literary reputation, perhaps more in 1831 than she had in 1816 when she first conceived of Victor Frankenstein's "workshop of filthy creation." After Percy Shelley's death she wrote prolifically, attempting to support her son, father, and even her stepsister, Claire Clairmont. Indeed, she was often exhausted by her writing. Yet convention dictated that she provide a decorous frame around *Frankenstein*—which had already been published in a "Standard Novels" edition—that made clear her position as a proper and widowed literary woman. Percy Shelley and Byron, whose reputations as major poets had continued to grow, along with their reputations as libertines, could help her bear the credit (and the blame) for *Frankenstein*'s "hideous" subject matter; she therefore calls upon them in her introduction to do so.

In the introduction Mary Shelley also reviews the scene of the monster's creation, this time providing details that would be emphasized in film versions to the exclusion of the more complex psychological issues suggested in the original scene: "I saw the hideous phantasm of a man stretched out, and then, on the working of some powerful engine, show signs of life, and stir with an uneasy, half-vital motion; for supremely frightful would be the effect of any human endeavour to mock the stupendous mechanism of the Creator of the world" (55). That this vision has become the standard focus of film versions of *Frankenstein* demonstrates how inseparable the introduction is from the novel. Notably, Mary Shelley conflates religion and technology ("the stupendous mechanism of the Creator of the world") here. The conflation exposes a pressure that seems not to have been part of her original waking dream. By 1831 various movements to bring God into the realm of science had gained considerable force.[3]

Finally, Mary Shelley bids her "hideous progeny go forth," deceptively referring to the period of its origin as "happy days when death and grief were but words which found no true echo in my heart" (56). In truth, they were days filled with extraordinary conflict, death, and remorse (as well, no doubt, as considerable joy) caused in part by her illegitimate marital position. She concludes the introduction with a parting falsehood: "The alterations I have made . . . are principally of style. I have changed no portion of the story nor introduced any new ideas or circumstances." As we know thanks to textual scholars like Anne Mellor, however, she did make changes in the text that alter family configurations and reinforce women's roles as moral guardians of the home.

Viewing the introduction as the last in a series of frames to be constructed around *Frankenstein*'s central scene of monstrous creation clarifies the direction Mary Shelley's attitudes toward cultural ethics were taking in the years of *Frankenstein*'s composition and transformations. The references to marital relationships in the various narratives surrounding the central scene elucidate the importance of those relationships in the cultural conversation. More truthfully than elsewhere in the introduction, Mary Shelley concludes that she has left "the core . . . untouched" and signs herself "M.W.S., London, 15, October, 1831" (56), a signature that anticipates the opening salutation of the novel proper. It seems that, by 1831, Mary Wollstonecraft Shelley had become, at least rhetorically, Margaret Walton Saville, the married woman in England who watches over the morals and decorum of *Frankenstein.*

5

The Civil Servant

Continue for the present to write to me. . . . I may receive your letters on some occasions when I need them most to support my spirits.
—Robert Walton to Margaret Saville (66)

The series of letters that frame the story of Victor Frankenstein and his monster come as a surprise to readers who, conditioned by film versions, expect to be immediately confronted with a mad scientist. But these letters, written by Robert Walton, the ambitious young explorer who is the first to hear Frankenstein's full confession, are strategically arranged so as to create a complex social context for the tale they recount. Furthermore, the woman who receives those letters, Walton's sister, is as important as her brother to an understanding of Mary Shelley's novel; for, it is she who "hears" the confessions of both men. The first character to be mentioned in *Frankenstein* is a married woman: "To Mrs. Saville, England." This initial greeting reads as much like the dedication of a novel as the salutation of a letter that it is actually meant to be. And, as we shall see, both its functions, as dedication and salutation, are important for reinforcing an attitude that, as

I see it, is implied throughout *Frankenstein:* the cultural doctrine that a balanced, civilized society requires the uniquely "feminine" influence of women, especially those who have been legitimately enfranchised through marriage, was promulgated with particular force throughout the nineteenth century. *Frankenstein* suggests that Mary Shelley succumbed to the force of that argument, but with misgivings (some acknowledged, others implied). Her qualified surrender to the camp of domestic feminism is encoded in the married characters and marriage relationships within her novel.

We get to know the absent married lady to whom *Frankenstein* is addressed exclusively through her brother, Robert Walton, who writes from various locations on his way to the North Pole. But the first clue to her significance is the prominently placed salutation itself, every aspect of which fits a design Mary Shelley carefully worked out. She saw fit to place this formal greeting immediately before the reader's eye because it is Mrs. Saville, or someone like her, who is meant to pass judgment on the fantastic tale to follow. Discovering what Mrs. Saville is like thus becomes paramount for a "qualified" reading of the text.

Even before we know her first name or her relationship to the correspondent, we know that she is a "Mrs.," a married woman. The prominence of that title almost begs us to assess this woman's position in terms of the laws and controversies about marriage current in Mary Shelley's society. In legal terms, according to Sir William Blackstone's tremendously influential *Commentaries on the Laws of England* (1765–69), the married woman's legal existence was "incorporated and consolidated into that of the husband; under whose wing, protection and *cover* she performs everything."[1] In effect, Blackstone declared the married woman's independent being legally nonexistent. Although his interpretation was flawed by not taking into account the various means then available for a married woman to protect her property rights, it was nonetheless widely accepted until the early nineteenth century and is still considered a classic legal text. Reinforcing the biblical notion of the married couple as "one flesh," Blackstone's commentary also tacitly sanctioned the traditional belief that, in return for protection, a woman should promote her husband's economic projects, political institutions, and so on. "Cover" is an appropriate choice of words to describe the husband's right and responsibility: rather than reinforcing the idea of marital *union,* it highlights the inequality inherent in marriage practices and incorporates the idea of protecting, shutting in, hiding, and preempting a territory.

The patronizing attitude implied in Blackstone's commentary carries tremendous weight even today. But, as outlined in the first chapter of this book, Mary Shelley's childhood was marked by a period of agitation *against* the marriage laws and against marriage itself. Even before Mary Shelley was born, Jeremy Bentham had criticized Blackstone's *Commentaries* in *A Fragment on Government* (1776) for the conservative view of marriage laws (among others) that Blackstone took. Her own father's *Political Justice* was one of the most frequently cited philosophical texts on the subject of marriage, and Percy Shelley's *Queen Mab* (1813) was one of the most controversial literary works expressing antimarriage sentiments. Her choice to make Margaret Saville a married woman, then, must be read as an informed decision to enter the controversy about the married woman's role. And considering the respect Mrs. Saville commands, we might assume, at the very least, Mary Shelley's qualified approval of that role.

Besides revealing the important fact that Mrs. Saville is married, her name suggests the idea of citizenship, for *sa ville,* French for "her town," might also be understood as a homonym for "civil." The extended meaning of Saville could then be construed to include all that pertains to the civilized life, especially as it is lived in France, in whose language Mrs. Saville's name is expressed, and in England, where (the salutation indicates) she resides. The French language, which Mary Shelley knew well, had long been recognized in England as the most civil and cultured of tongues. Furthermore, it was the language of the country where the egalitarian principles of her mother, father, and future husband had been radically advocated. Ironically, though, following the French Revolution the middle-class married woman's place became even more restricted in France than in England. Auguste Comte, the influential French philosopher whose life span closely matches Mary Shelley's, and whose influence was strongest in England and France, "declared that there were radical differences, physical and moral, between male and female which separated them profoundly. . . . Femininity was a kind of 'prolonged infancy' that set woman aside from 'the ideal of the race' and enfeebled her mind. He foresaw the total abolition of female labor outside the home. In morality and love woman might be set up as superior, but man acted, while she remained in the home without economic or political rights."[2]

Judging from the clues her brother provides, Margaret Saville, probably French by marriage if not by birth, has been "set up" according to Comtean guidelines. His separate-sphere philosophy for men and women was widely argued throughout Western culture in the eighteenth and nineteenth centuries, and Margaret Saville, both in name and in function, clearly resides in a sphere of influence separate from that of the men in the novel.

In a study arguing that Mary Shelley meant to promote an androgynous philosophy in *Frankenstein,* William Veeder also notes Margaret Saville's significance in the novel. Veeder asserts that Margaret Saville has "been seriously undervalued by critics." He further implies that Mary Shelley may have meant us to translate "Margaret" into its original Greek meaning of "pearl" (82); doing so, I would point out, renders her a cultivated adornment to society rather than an active participant in it. On the other hand, Margaret is also a rather common English name, with Middle English roots, and the given name of a famous sixteenth-century woman writer Mary Shelley admired, Queen Margaret of Navarre. Reading Mrs. Saville as a cultured but influential and talented woman philosophically poised among countries believed to be the most advanced civilizations of the Western world, we might conclude that Mary Shelley, her creator, held married women uniquely responsible for maintaining the philosophical balance of society.

Any tenet that holds married women to be in some sense special seems at odds with the facts of Mary Shelley's marital history up until the conception of *Frankenstein.* Nonetheless, the married woman's role is idealized throughout the novel, beginning with Margaret Walton Saville. Surely it is no accident that Margaret's initials, M.W.S., are the very ones Mary anticipated acquiring for herself when she decided to introduce her story of monstrous creation with a series of letters to a married woman. Attempting to influence her brother's behavior through her writing, Margaret Saville becomes one with Mary Shelley, who similarly intends to influence the reader. Each woman thus assumes the role of civil servant and, in effect, becomes both the ideal reader—the kind of reader Mary Shelley wished for her novel—and the shaper of *Frankenstein.*

We know *that* Margaret Saville writes, because scattered throughout the opening letters of *Frankenstein* are her brother's direct responses to what she has said. Those responses disclose much about what Margaret has written, what she previously has taught her brother, and therefore much about her nature. Early on we learn that she has regarded Walton's enterprise with "evil forebodings" (59). Furthermore, Walton seems to expect that she will "contest the inestimable benefit [he] shall confer on all mankind to the last generation, by discovering a passage near the pole . . . or by ascertaining the secret of the magnet" (60). Clearly, she is not enthusiastic about his latest obsession. Nonetheless, after recalling the various frustrated enthusiasms of his youth—with which his sister is already acquainted—Walton asks for Margaret's approval: "Do I not deserve to accomplish some great purpose?" he asks (61). But the negative construction of Walton's question prompts us to surmise once again Margaret's judgmental and doubting frame of mind, even as it confirms Walton's respect for her opinion. Walton's second letter further implies Margaret's lack of sympathy with his "romantic" leanings and makes clear his desire for a friend who, unlike Margaret, will share his dreams: "You may deem me romantic, my dear sister, but I bitterly feel the want of a friend [to] repair the faults of your poor brother . . . who would have sense enough not to despise me as romantic" (63–64).

Further along, Walton admits that his "best years" had been spent under her "gentle and feminine fosterage," which "has so refined the groundwork of my character that I cannot overcome an intense distaste for the usual brutality exercised on board ship" (64). This passage did not appear in the original version of *Frankenstein;* its inclusion in the final version supports the likelihood that Mary Shelley had become increasingly convinced that woman's proper role in a smoothly functioning society was to be the molder of character, taste, and morality. To that end, the ideal woman was to become widely educated and cultivated. Mary Shelley's mother had advocated a similar script in *The Rights of Woman,* but in 1831 the doctrine that Mary Wollstonecraft had hoped would liberate women was being reinterpreted to keep them in their domestic place. That place was a sphere of influence complementary to but decidedly separate from the public arena that men "naturally" inhabited. Margaret Saville's position in *Frankenstein* demonstrates the persuasiveness of this latter-day distortion of Mary Wollstonecraft's philosophy, a distortion that Wollstonecraft herself may have invited in assertions like: "Make women rational creatures, and free citizens, and they will quickly become good wives and mothers."[3]

The separate-sphere philosophy was so seductive and powerful that it retains tremendous appeal even today. It was perfectly articulated in the writings of Catherine Beecher, an internationally respected New England educator of the early nineteenth century. I will quote Beecher at some length so that the reader may experience the seductive rhetoric Mary Shelley herself would have been exposed to. The stand Beecher takes is pertinent not only to Margaret Saville but to all the women in *Frankenstein:*

> Woman is to win everything by peace and love; by making herself so much respected, esteemed and loved, that to yield to her opinions and to gratify her wishes, will be the free-will offering of the heart. But this is to be all accomplished in the domestic and social circle. There let every woman become so cultivated and refined in intellect, that her taste and judgement will be respected; so benevolent in feeling and action; that her motives will be reverenced;— so unassuming and unambitious, that collision and competition will be banished;—so "gentle and easy to be entreated," as that every heart will repose in her presence; then, the fathers, the husbands, and the sons, will find an influence thrown around them, to which they will yield not only willingly but proudly. A man is never ashamed to own such influences, but feels dignified and ennobled in acknowledging them. But the moment the woman begins to feel the promptings of ambition, or the thirst for power, her aegis of defence is gone.[4]

Although Mary Shelley apparently meant to expose the disastrous consequences of Victor Frankenstein's turning his back on the sort of feminine influence Beecher describes, we shall see that the novel—perhaps inadvertently—also reproaches women for following Beecher's prescription too closely. While Margaret Saville seems to fare well as civil servant, the fates of Justine and Elizabeth dramatically underscore the failings of the separate-sphere philosophy.

In the letter in which Walton recalls Margaret's "gentle and feminine fosterage" he also recounts the story of a mariner he has recently met who both attracts and repels him. Again, Walton's reaction to the mariner, and his prediction of Margaret's response, reveal much about his teacher and highlight her philosophical kinship with the likes of Catherine Beecher. The mariner in question generously leaves the country and stays away until he hears that the resistant young woman who had been promised him in marriage by her father has instead been "married according to her inclinations": " 'What a noble fellow!' you will exclaim. He is so; but then he is wholly uneducated: he is as silent as a Turk, and a kind of ignorant carelessness attends him, which, while it renders his conduct the more astonishing detracts from the interest and sympathy he otherwise would command" (65). The fact that Walton readily anticipates Margaret's response indicates that he knows her preferences well. He knows, for example, that she will approve the mariner's insistence that the young woman be allowed to marry the man of her choice; Margaret thereby takes a stand, in absentia, against the custom of arranged marriages still prevalent in England and France. But, from the phrase "he is wholly uneducated" to the end of the passage, Walton's description of the mariner exposes a simple, quiet, unassuming man of whom he is sure Margaret will *not* fully approve. Margaret's as well as Walton's prejudice against the uneducated "lower" classes is thus revealed. This passage, added for the final version of the novel, indicates that Mary Shelley's attitude of acceptance of the conventional training and attitudes of a middle-class, civilized woman had become more clearly and precisely formulated by 1831 than it had been in 1818.

We may also learn from Walton's direct references to Margaret's feelings how effective she had been as his early childhood teacher; her gentle fosterage had left its impression on him. Indeed, one of the con-

ciliatory gestures to women seeking political equality in the early nineteenth century was excessive emphasis on their function as teachers
during children's formative years. One historian of the period, Jane
Lewis, sees this emphasis as a major strand in nineteenth-century feminism, which accepted and attempted to expand the idea of "women as
the natural guardians of the moral order." The nineteenth-century
feminist Josephine Butler summarized the notion by describing the
home as the "nursery of all virtue."[5] Based on these attitudes to
women's formative role in the home, we might assume that whatever
virtues Walton ultimately demonstrates are attributable to Margaret's
influence.

In spite of minor complaints and his want of a sympathetic
friend, Walton vows not to waver in his resolution. However, he continues, "you know me sufficiently to confide in my prudence and considerateness whenever the safety of others is committed to my care"
(65). This reassuring promise made to the one person whose judgment
still seems most important to him will be honored, but with great difficulty. He will be sorely tempted by the example of Victor Frankenstein
to forget his sister's lessons and sacrifice his little shipboard community
to the achievement of a rather questionable higher good. In honoring
his commitment to the crew, however, Walton will set himself apart
from Victor Frankenstein and, "ennobled," as Catherine Beecher
would say, by Margaret's early influence, will have served his community well.

Walton's succeeding invocation of *The Rime of the Ancient
Mariner* reinforces both the exploratory nature of his quest and the
theme of responsibility to the community that Margaret's involvement
emphasizes. This second reference to a mariner is historically as well as
literarily apt because it focuses attention on myriad issues being
debated during the period 1818–31. One questionable issue was
England's expanding colonial imperialism. As the century wore on,
and more men left home to contribute to the expansion of the empire,
it would be increasingly difficult for women to fulfill their circumscribed roles as moral guardians.

Coleridge's poem, so impressive to Mary Shelley when as a child
she heard the poet himself recite it, had in the intervening years been

overshadowed by the works of Byron, Shelley, and Keats. The *Ancient Mariner's* ethical, even religious, anti-individualist theme in many ways opposes later romantic ideals. But even though the *Ancient Mariner* is not specifically about women's roles, it emphasizes a moral that women especially were asked to reinforce with increasing vigor. Ironically, as women responded to demands that they be guardians of the moral order, Mariner-like transgressions of communal taboos among explorers and colonists were being perpetrated and even rewarded in legally sanctioned extensions of the British Empire as, for instance, the East India Company. Incidences of shipboard brutality, such as Walton alludes to, were often reported in connection with these imperialist ventures. Thus the reference to *The Rime of the Ancient Mariner*, another 1831 addition to Frankenstein, is rendered extraordinarily appropriate in historical terms. It underscores the difficult position of a woman like Margaret, who is expected to oversee the morals of her brother even when she is excluded from his outbound ship.

As Walton moves away from his sister's sphere of influence, his confidence about his mission seems to grow. Again anticipating her corrective admonitions, he first reassures her: "Be assured that for my own sake, as well as yours, I will not rashly encounter danger. I will be cool, persevering, and prudent." But he abruptly takes a different tone, challenging and almost defiant: "But success *shall* crown my endeavours. . . . What can stop the determined heart and resolved will of man?" (67–68). Primed for adventure in a world uninhabited by women, he soon meets the sympathetic friend he has longed for.

Walton's fourth letter describes his momentous meeting with Victor Frankenstein, who is in many ways Margaret Saville's opposite number. An unmarried man, in pursuit of a "daemon," far from his own country, Victor Frankenstein seems to be the nemesis of civil society as represented by Margaret. Once Walton meets this "brother of [his] heart" (72), the salutations to Margaret cease and his direct responses to her become more condescending. Mary Shelley added a paragraph for the 1831 edition that reinforces this change in Walton's attitude, again calling attention to Margaret's separate sphere of influence and clearly exposing its limitations: "Will you smile at the enthusiasm I express concerning this divine wanderer? You would not if you saw him. You have been tutored and refined by books and retirement from the world, and you are therefore somewhat fastidious; but this only renders you the more fit to appreciate the extraordinary merits of this wonderful man" (74). The inherent contradictions in the arguments of social philosophers like Auguste Comte and Catherine Beecher are obvious here in Walton's letter. Comte, Beecher, and Robert Walton all attempt to elevate middle-class women to the status of civil guardians while keeping them in their domestic places. If, on the one hand, Margaret is tutored, refined, and retired *from* the world, how can she be "more fit to appreciate" this "divine wanderer" who is decidedly out *in* the world? This conflict between women's responsibility to maintain the moral order and their limited opportunities to do so is unresolved in the remainder of *Frankenstein*. But recognition of it is central to an understanding of the antagonisms between Victor Frankenstein, his Creature, and Victor's family.

The final series of letters, recorded in chapter 24, underscores even more dramatically the untenable nature of the separate-sphere doctrine. Walton becomes intoxicated by Victor Frankenstein's rallying cry to the crew: "Do not return to your families with the stigma of disgrace marked on your brows. Return as heroes who have fought and conquered and who know not what it is to turn their backs on the foe" (253). This speech is nothing more than a series of powerful, "heroic," but nonetheless empty clichés. Under their control, Walton seems not to consider that there is in fact no "foe," and certainly no disgrace in turning back from a dangerous and rather ambiguous venture. In the throes of a typically masculinist quest for glory, and egged on by Victor Frankenstein, the master quester, Walton resentfully agrees to turn back. "The die is cast: I have consented to return if we are not destroyed. Thus are my hopes blasted by cowardice and indecision; I come back ignorant and disappointed. It requires more philosophy than I possess to bear this injustice with patience" (254). Walton has clearly forgotten his earlier assurances to Margaret. Speaking in *her* terms, he had referred to his "prudence and considerateness whenever the safety of others" was concerned. But what is deemed prudent and considerate in Margaret's sphere has become "cowardice and indecision" in the quintessentially male sphere of *his*

Arctic expedition. Subsequently, Walton promises to further recount the details of his failed quest to Margaret, "and while I am wafted toward England and towards you I will not despond" (254). It is apparent in this closing letter that only a very thin thread connects Walton to Margaret's world. Her early fosterage has barely rescued him from the seductions of Victor Frankenstein's sphere of influence.

Mary Shelley has thus carefully designed these framing letters between Robert Walton and Margaret Saville, the "civil servant" of the novel and her own surrogate, to establish the complicated ethical problems inherent in a society that advocated separate spheres of influence for men and women.

6

Minor Rites

> The circumstances of his marriage relate his character.
> —Victor Frankenstein, discussing his father (76)

The major narratives of *Frankenstein* feature cameo appearances by couples who evidence Mary Shelley's growing conviction that strong marriage ties, though restrictive, are necessary to civilized society, and who reveal her developing image of the ideal male-female partnership. The behavior of the individuals in these minor parts testifies not only to their value as humane beings but also to Mary Shelley's reluctant approval of their complementary, although separate and necessarily unequal role assignments. Paradoxically, the extreme of such sexual division of labor is Victor Frankenstein's cutting himself off from feminine influences at home in order to create the monster. Thus in Victor's case the separate-sphere philosophy is exposed as a radically divisive, destructive force in the culture. The 1831 text suggests, however, that Mary Shelley intended to denounce only the extreme of that philosophy while upholding the principle itself.

Mary Shelley's tenuous emotional and financial situation from the day she eloped with Percy Shelley until their son inherited the Shelley fortune made her particularly susceptible to the ideal of the middle-class woman, protected and respected, living in a financially secure and peaceful environment. Of necessity she wrote and published prolifically during those years to support her family. But she longed for relief. A journal entry of 8 March 1831 conveys her turmoil: "Here gaunt poverty & cruel privation dog my pleasures close—cares beset me—& fair expectations die—Could I concenter my affections round a home I should ask no more—the luxuries of wea[l]th are nothing to me—I ask only a home with one or two who would . . . find the solace of their life in my care and affection—but this is denied me—& I am miserable beyond words" (*Journals,* 520). The male-female partnerships in *Frankenstein* reflect Mary Shelley's frame of mind. In some ways they act as wish fulfillments, dispelling her resentment and frustration. But they also expose problems in the developing roles of married men and women in the culture at large that she was perfectly aware of. Furthermore, the novel's subtly variant nineteenth-century middle-class marriage patterns reveal nearly all the more general cultural concerns about reforming English society politically and economically.

Of the emblematic marriages embedded in *Frankenstein,* the most fully developed is that of Victor Frankenstein's parents. The bare facts of the senior Frankensteins' union reveal a well-to-do, middle-aged politician who, in retirement, marries the impoverished, beautiful, considerably younger daughter of a deceased old friend. (A modified Cinderella tale if there ever was one.) Immediately after the death of Caroline Beaufort's father, Alphonse Frankenstein had come "like a protecting spirit to the poor girl, who committed herself to his care" (77). Two years later they marry, and Alphonse strives "to shelter her, as a fair exotic is sheltered by the gardener, from every rougher wind, and to surround her with all that could tend to excite pleasurable emotion in her soft and benevolent mind" (78). Blackstone's legal commentaries, making of the husband a protective "cover" for his wife, and Catherine Beecher's formula for feminine behavior, designating the wife a "cultivated and refined" domestic, are both echoed in this passage. But Caroline Beaufort Frankenstein is only the most clearly defined of numerous women characters in *Frankenstein* described as "fair," "exotic," "soft," and "benevolent" female partners.

While the separate-sphere design for women reproduced in the Alphonse Frankenstein household closely matches the Catherine Beecher model, the pattern advocated for men, as epitomized in Alphonse, is somewhat enlarged. He has operated in the public domain *before* marriage so that *after* marriage he can devote time and attention to his wife and children. In fact, this arrangement allows him to participate in both the masculine and feminine spheres of influence: "He was respected by all who knew him for his integrity and indefatigable attention to public business. . . . Nor was it until the decline of life that he became a husband and the father of a family" (76). After marriage, in his "decline," Alphonse becomes so devoted a husband that he takes up Caroline's interests to the extent that the two seem to become one: "*Their* benevolent disposition often made them enter the cottages of the poor" (78; emphasis mine). But, in fact, these charitable ministrations had always meant more to Caroline than to Alphonse; indeed, they were to her, as politics had been to him, "a necessity, a passion" (79). Moreover, we soon learn that Alphonse did not always accompany his wife on these visits; one might infer from Victor's account that Alphonse's retirement from public affairs was not as complete as Victor would have had us originally believe. "One day," Victor notes, "when my father had gone by himself to Milan, my mother, accompanied by me, visited [a poor cottage]" (79). The result of this visit is that Caroline, without consulting her husband, adopts Elizabeth, the daughter she had always wanted, thus relegitimizing and enlarging her own domestic role. She will enlarge her circle of influence again when she later takes the ill-fated Justine Moritz into the Frankenstein home.

While Alphonse crosses gender-determined borders of social activity, then, Caroline, although expanding her domain, remains severely circumscribed. Completely uninvolved in public affairs and ignorant of her father's economic situation before his ruin, Caroline Beaufort had been schooled in the "gentler" arts. For a brief period, when her father's failure had demanded it, she had shown an enterprising side by plaiting straw. But this activity seems to have been, like Penelope's weaving as she awaited Odysseus's return and retirement from military life, merely a way of marking time until her rescuer appeared.

Victor Frankenstein casually discounts the age difference between his parents: "There was a considerable difference between the ages of my parents, but this circumstance seemed to unite them only closer in bonds of devoted affection" (77). In fact, considerable age difference between marriage partners of the middle and upper classes was perfectly acceptable in the nineteenth century. Nonetheless, it created a *real*, though largely unacknowledged barrier between the partners that reinforced the artificial boundaries erected to define male and female roles. Both physical vigor and life experiences separated May-December marriage partners like the Alphonse Frankensteins, emphasizing the inequities that the law guaranteed and making it unlikely that they could be fully sympathetic to one another's needs or occupations.

Yet, if we accept Victor Frankenstein's assessment of his parents' marriage, it was ideal. That assessment is, of course, colored by his experience of them as parents. Before his adopted sister Elizabeth Lavenza and his brother William entered the family, Victor had been the only darling of his parents: "Much as they were attached to each other, they seemed to draw inexhaustible stores of affection . . . to bestow them upon me. . . . I was their plaything and their idol, and something better—their child, the innocent and helpless creature bestowed on them by heaven . . . to direct to happiness or misery, according as they fulfilled their duties toward me" (78). Encoded in this description of Victor Frankenstein's early childhood is a combination of several contending nineteenth-century philosophies about appropriate parent-child relationships. Here we see an extremely sentimental view of the absolutely innocent child combined with the notion that parents are not only required to educate that child but will be called to account for the child's future happiness or misery. Mary Shelley very likely intended this passage to provide a contrast to Victor Frankenstein's later mistreatment of *his* "child," the Creature. But it also incorporates issues that her own parents had confronted in their roles as educational philosophers, and that she herself had been facing while raising and educating her son.

Both William Godwin and Mary Wollstonecraft believed early childhood to be the time when an individual's values are formed. Although that principle is now considered a given, in Mary Shelley's world it was still arguable. Even more arguable were the questions of how involved or indulgent parents should be in helping to form their children's values, and which parent should provide what sort of influence.

Although both rejected the idea of a highly structured course of study or abusive physical discipline for a child, Mary Shelley's parents agreed that a child should *not* be treated as a "plaything" or left without direction. Nor should a child be worshiped as an "idol." Rather, one's offspring should be respected as an intelligent being and encouraged from an early age to develop "moral faculties." Such development could be brought about by exposing the child to a wide variety of imaginative written works that would provide vicarious experiences for dealing with human conflict. Both regarded as harmful to the culture the growing tendency to rate scientific study higher than the humanities. William Godwin summed up his philosophy of education in his preface to *Bible Stories,* published in 1802: "Imagination is the characteristic of man. The dexterities of logic or of mathematical deduction belong rather to a well regulated machine; they do not contain in them the living principle of our nature. It is the heart which most deserves to be cultivated; not the rules which may serve us in the nature of a compass to steer through the difficulties of life; but the pulses which beat with sympathy, and qualify us for the habits of charity, reverence, and attachment" (St. Clair, 280). As benign as Victor paints them, the educational methods of the senior Frankensteins do not measure up to these principles that Mary Shelley was raised by and to which she subscribed throughout her life. Neither in early childhood nor in his later education does Victor Frankenstein seem to have been firmly guided toward concerns of the "heart." Furthermore, in Victor's later studies his mother seems to be completely absent as an influence, and Victor implies that Alphonse's guidance is minimal:

"My father looked carelessly at the title page of my book and said, 'Ah! Cornelius Agrippa! My dear Victor, do not waste your time upon this; it is sad trash.' If, instead of this remark, my father had taken the pains to explain to me that the principles of Agrippa had been entirely exploded . . . I should certainly have thrown Agrippa aside. . . . But the cursory glance my father had taken of my volume by no means assured me that he was acquainted with its contents" (83–84).

By including such apparently inconsequential but revealing observations as these in his own "irrevocably . . . determined" history (75), Victor suggests that early excessive pampering and later lack of educational guidance in the home are partly responsible for his self-indulgent obsession with bringing into the world a Creature he cannot possibly love. Accordingly, we might take as ominous his declaration that "no human being could have passed a happier childhood than myself. My parents were possessed by the very spirit of kindness and indulgence" (82).

Here and there before Victor's quintessential act of self-indulgence in animating the Creature the dire consequences of his own spoiling are predicted: "The lives of my parents were passed in considerable seclusion. It was my temper to avoid a crowd and to attach myself fervently to a few. . . . I was indifferent to my schoolfellows in general" (81); "My temper was sometimes violent, and my passions vehement" (82).

Since Alphonse Frankenstein had put his political activities behind him before marriage, Victor had not witnessed firsthand any of the altruistic projects his father may have undertaken. His visiting the poor, an act of charity largely relegated to women, was done primarily in deference to his wife. Aside from these visits, Caroline herself was devoted entirely to her family, especially the children, thus perfectly fulfilling the role of domestic angel while neglecting any individual talents she may have had. Meanwhile, as the family moved "more than a league from the city" (81), to where the complex ethical problems indigenous to urban areas impinged less frequently on their consciousness, Victor's education tended more and more to the abstract, "heartless" sciences: "I confess that neither the structure of languages, nor the code of governments, nor the politics of various states possessed attractions for me. It was the secrets of heaven and earth that I desired to learn; and whether it was the outward substance of things or the inner spirit of nature and the mysterious soul of man that occupied me, still my enquiries were directed to the metaphysical, or in its highest sense, the physical secrets of the world" (82). In contrast to Victor's preoccupations, his friend Clerval's interests lay "with the moral relations of things" (82). Along with Clerval, Elizabeth serves to counter Victor's tendencies to be too metaphysical and abstract in his concerns. "She was the living spirit of love to soften and attract; I might have become sullen in my study, rough through the ardour of my nature, but that she was there to subdue me to a semblance of her own gentleness" (83). As Margaret Saville had done for Robert Walton, Elizabeth refines Victor's nature in these early years. It is important to note, too, that just as Margaret Saville must later attempt to exert her civilizing influence from her home in England, Elizabeth enters Victor's philosophical and professional world only by way of her letters. She is expected to and does provide an overlay of humaneness to his sensibilities as long as he is at home. Once Victor leaves, however, the influence of his mother, Elizabeth, and Clerval is nearly extinguished. The question of Elizabeth's failed relationship with Victor is particularly important to an understanding of his monstrous act of creation, and I will consider that subject in detail in chapter 7.

It is the speciously harmonious relationship of his parents, however, that provides Victor's first exposure to a culturally approved, apparently ideal marital union. The real dysfunction of that union shows itself in its product, Victor, who seems incapable of genuine unselfish love in spite of his surface cultivation and sensibility. Notably, Alphonse Frankenstein takes on his wife's nurturing role *after* her death: "My father's care and attentions were indefatigable" (225). While she was alive, however, the two had more or less kept their assigned places.

The relationship of Alphonse and Caroline establishes a model of marital behavior, although a flawed one, to which others in the novel might be compared. Elizabeth's father, a ruined Milanese nobleman and political activist, puts Elizabeth out for adoption when his wife dies, never doubting the conventional wisdom that child rearing is primarily a feminine occupation (79). On the other hand, Justine

Moritz's father had favored her, but "through a strange perversity, her mother could not endure her and after the death of M. Moritz, treated her very ill" (109). The parents of Safie, the beautiful young Arab who brings such joy into the De Lacey home, are also out of sync. Her father is a "treacherous Turk" (167) who attempts to control her choices, while her mother, a Christian Arab who has "spurned the bondage to which she is now reduced" (165), encourages Safie's independent spirit.

Of all the couples in *Frankenstein,* Safie and Felix come the closest, perhaps, to Mary Shelley's ideal of what a relationship should be. However, it seems significant that although we are led to believe they eventually will, they do not marry in the novel. Before Safie arrives on the scene, the Creature observes that Felix is the "saddest" member of his family and seems to "suffer more deeply" than the other De Laceys (154). Yet, although he displays a sorrowful countenance (we later learn that both his poverty and his separation from Safie cause his despondency), he maintains a cheerful tone of voice for the benefit of his blind father. He is "slight and graceful in his figure" (150) and, along with his sister, Agatha, "appeared to weep" (152). We thus learn that he is a man who has all the sensitivity and even some physical characteristics a woman might be expected to have. Safie's arrival utterly transforms him, and this emblematic reunion clarifies the quality of their relationship: "Felix seemed ravished with delight when he saw her, every trait of sorrow vanished from his face, and it instantly expressed a degree of ecstatic joy, of which I could hardly have believed it capable; his eyes sparkled, as his cheek flushed with pleasure; and at that moment I thought him as beautiful as the stranger. She appeared affected by different feelings; wiping a few tears from her lovely eyes, she held out her hand to Felix" (158–59). The observation that Safie "appeared affected by different feelings" than Felix implies that she may be responding to this emotionally charged reunion less extravagantly than Felix and therefore more like a man. Felix appears "as beautiful as" Safie to the Creature in this scene, further reinforcing the idea that the two have entered each other's gender-determined domains. Finally, Safie sends a double message: "wiping a few tears from her eyes . . . she held out her hand to Felix" is a gesture that combines feminine emotionalism with masculine restraint.

The history of Felix's relationship with Safie—he provides a means of escape from France for Safie's father and pays for his benevolence with his own family's imprisonment and impoverishment—reveals that he is not only sensitive but courageous, resourceful, and committed to egalitarian principles. These are all virtues Percy Shelley possessed. Mary Shelley may very well have had Percy Shelley at his most impulsively generous in mind when she created Felix, just as she had her lover's darker, obsessive, egoistic tendencies in mind when she created Victor Frankenstein.

Safie proves to be in every way worthy of Felix. Though a minor character in *Frankenstein*, it is clear from her impact on both the De Laceys and the Creature that she clarifies an important "meaning" of *Frankenstein:* society must make talented, educated women indispensable to the family and the culture or else it is doomed. As Felix is likely to be an idealized version of Percy Shelley, so Safie seems to represent Mary Shelley's exemplary alter ego. Breaking the mold advocated by Catherine Beecher, she closely resembles the vindicated woman Mary Wollstonecraft had described earlier. She is taught by her mother, as Mary Shelley had been, "to aspire to higher powers of intellect and an independence of spirit" (165). Safie, who appears to be about his age, also demonstrates courage and resourcefulness equal to Felix's. Escaping her father's restrictions, she ventures into a land where she cannot even speak the language, hoping for greater opportunities to fulfill her potential. With a hint of "masculine" opportunism that seems to dilute the strength of her affection for Felix, Safie finds the "prospect of marrying a Christian and remaining in a country where women were allowed to take a rank in society" enchanting (166).

As with Margaret Saville, Safie's very name elicits a rich composite of personalities and meanings that helps us evaluate her character. The Arabic word *safi,* which translates as "purity," was the surname of the ruling Persian dynasty from 1500 to 1736, while the Greek *sophia* means "wisdom." Sophia was also a favorite British name for the heroines of popular early novels. In Henry Fielding's *Tom Jones* (1749), for example, the spirited young Sophia Western (affectionately known as

"Sophy") runs away from her father, much as Safie does, because he refuses to let her marry her disinherited lover. Safie's name therefore incorporates the nineteenth-century British interest in the exotic East, respect for feminine purity and wisdom, and pride in the respectable but sporting middle-class female character.

Safie's name and character, as well as Felix's character, are also likely to have been derived partly from Mary Shelley's reading during 1815–16. For several weeks in September 1816 she reread selected works of Jean Jacques Rousseau. His *Emile* (1762), a treatise on education addressed to mothers, features Sophie, a well-born young woman who marries Emile, a French orphan who is her intellectual superior. But, as her mother had done in *The Rights of Woman*, Mary Shelley apparently uses the story of Safie and Felix to challenge Rousseau's representation of unequal male-female capacities.

In addition to *Emile*, Mary Shelley also reread Rousseau's *Julie, ou la Nouvelle Héloïse* during this period. An epistolary, semiautobiographical novel, it recounts the story of Julie, a young woman torn between love for her tutor and duty to her father, who has arranged a marriage for her. The parallels between Julie, Safie, and Mary Shelley herself are obvious. But unlike Rousseau's heroine, who respects her father's wishes, Mary Shelley and Safie, her fictional alter ego, choose the love of their tutors over their fathers' dicta.

Safie cleverly escapes her father's control and the vicissitudes of the harem for the relative freedom of the De Lacey cottage. There she proves her worth both by thriving under Felix's able tutelage and by returning a measure of the financial security the family lost when Felix had championed her father. She brings unparalleled joy into the household with her exquisite beauty and musical talent. In fact, she seems to occupy precisely the position Mary Shelley described in her journal: "I ask only a home with one or two who would . . . find the solace of their life in my care and affection" (Journals, 520).

Anne Mellor, too, sees Safie as one of several Mary Shelley heroines who projects an ideal suggested in her mother's works, an individualist who yet contributes significantly to the welfare of an egalitarian bourgeois family (Mellor, 209, 214). Safie's legal position in the De Lacey family never becomes quite clear, however. And while her relationship with Felix seems more balanced than other male-female couplings in the novel, we are left with the impression that she gets disproportionate attention in the family. What's more, her unmitigated physical perfection, like Caroline Beaufort's and Elizabeth Lavenza's, belong to the conventions of a fairy tale rather than to real life.

Since we are viewing Safie and Felix through the eyes of the Creature, one might argue that we are getting his biased representation of the couple, a picture that overstates Safie's influence. Nonetheless, this intriguing, young, nearly married couple may represent Mary Shelley's hopes and uncertainties about her future with Percy Shelley, as well as about the possibility of truly egalitarian relationships in the culture generally.

7

Unbridled Affections

The wretch saw me destroy the creature on whose future existence
he depended for happiness, and with a howl of devilish despair and
revenge, withdrew.

—Victor Frankenstein (207)

Nothing in *Frankenstein* is more unexpected than the Creature's sensitivity. Victor Frankenstein's account of his Creature up to chapter 11
represents a hideous, violent, thoroughly abhorrent being. But from
the beginning of his own tale, as he awakes to "the operation of [his]
various senses" (144), to the conclusion, when he demands that Victor
create a being "as deformed and horrible" as himself (185), the
Creature reveals an unusual capacity for both self-analysis and compassion. Even Victor is moved by the Creature's story and finds that
the "tale and the feelings he . . . expressed proved him to be a creature
of fine sensations" (187). Except when he has been driven by rejection
to seek revenge, the Creature naturally balances healthy egoism and
selfless altruism. While these qualities bring to mind both the hypo-
thetical "natural man" promoted by Rousseau in *Discours sur l'origine
de l'inégalité* and the ideal communal man suggested in William

Godwin's *Political Justice,* the Creature's decidedly self-reflexive nature has also led some critics to believe that Mary Shelley invested much of her own personality in this complex character. As Safie projects the image of Mary Shelley's ideal public self, the Creature seems to reflect her deepest sensitivity, confusion, guilt, and anger.

A motherless, self-educated, close observer of human behavior, the Creature has been rejected by his "father" and desperately seeks an intimate, enduring relationship with sympathetic beings. Viewed in these terms, he could easily be Mary Shelley's alter ego. Other characteristics support this parallel. Like Mary Shelley, he is an excellent and enthusiastic student. Given his startling ability to draw logical conclusions from what he patiently observes and reads, he is a better student than the impulsive Victor ever was: "I was at first unable to solve these questions [about the De Lacey family's sadness] but perpetual attention and time explained to me many appearances which were at first enigmatic" (153). Less egocentric and more desirous of human companionship than Victor, he is also, like Mary Shelley, a more authentic, practical humanitarian: "This trait of kindness moved me sensibly. . . . I discovered also another means through which I was enabled to assist their labours. I . . . brought home firing sufficient for the consumption of several days" (153). Rather than the overblown, abstract philanthropy Victor Frankenstein professes—"A new species would bless me as its creator and source; many happy and excellent natures would owe their being to me" (97)—the Creature sees that his adopted family has a pressing need for fuel and simply takes care of it. He frequently weeps, as, for example, when he "wept with Safie over the hapless fate" of America's "original inhabitants" (161). He hopes to win over the De Lacey family by his "gentle demeanour and conciliating words," characteristics typically defined as feminine.

Foiled in his attempts to gain even a minimum return on his affections, however, the Creature seeks revenge in physical violence. Here the comparison with Mary Shelley seems most obviously to break down. Yet the Creature's violent behavior compares to the fantasies of revenge that occur to even the most civilized of beings when they feel wronged and frustrated. Just prior to and during the composition of *Frankenstein,* Mary Shelley was feeling rejected and thwarted in her attempts to form a perfect union of her father, Shelley, their relatives, and herself, and she understandably experienced psychological stress. That stress might have been somewhat relieved by imaginary acts of revenge; but, ironically, even imaginary violence can render a fundamentally ethical person guilty. Guilt for entertaining fantasies of revenge coupled with guilt for leaving her father's home to elope with another woman's husband could easily have made Mary seem a monster in her own eyes.

Indeed, by the time she conceived of her "ghost story," Mary had heard the current rumors about the sordid incestuous behavior of the group of young literary artists at the Villa Diodati. Thus Mary realized that others, too, may have judged her a monster of depravity. Writing *Frankenstein* and creating a sensitive monster, then, may have been a way of exorcising her private demons while proving her talent to the significant men in her life.

Keeping in mind the possibility that Mary Shelley was herself the inspiration for the Creature, it is notable that much of the Creature's distress is caused by his position as an outlaw. He exists *outside* the laws of nature and of man, illegitimate in every sense of the word. His illegitimacy as much as his ugliness makes him unacceptable in society. If his "father," Victor, had claimed and recognized him as the original of his kind instead of rejecting him because of his ugliness, the Creature would at least have had a place, a status and history from which he could have been judged and even appreciated and protected. Instead he has been denied even the meager security and companionship conceded such freaks of nature as are found in traveling shows. They at least belong to a community and operate within the rules of the carnival system.

With no legitimate outlet for his needs or affections, the monster eventually becomes unrestrained, uncontrolled, unbridled. Thus, in demanding a *bride*, a "companion . . . of the same species [with] the same defects" (185), the Creature seeks not only a loving mate but also a "bridle," a check on his passions that will both restrain and direct him. "The love of another will destroy the cause of my crimes. . . . I shall feel the affections of a sensitive being and become linked to the chain of existence and events from which I am now excluded"

(188–89). Here, in the Creature's demand for security and affection through union with a sympathetic being of similar kind, another analogy to Mary Shelley's life is suggested. Mary's relationship with Percy Shelley from 1814 to 1816 was illegitimate—outside the law—and unrestrained in the sense that it was not subject to the rules of middle-class marriage. Her children were also illegitimate and would very likely be verbally if not physically abused in a world where they would be social outcasts. As her relationship with Shelley progressed, it became more and more clear that its illegality would prevent Mary from ever achieving any financial security, social approval, or peace of mind for herself or her children. She longed for a more secure bond with Percy Shelley even though, publicly, they both continued to disdain the legal institution of marriage. However, Mary's conservative sexual behavior after Percy Shelley's death indicates that she eventually became uncomfortable with the liberated lifestyle into which her romance with him had drawn her. She was never to become involved in such unconventional living arrangements again.

Mary's (often repressed) dissatisfaction with the chaotic living conditions of her liaison was made more intense by her father's stubborn rejection of her union up until the time she became Percy Shelley's legal wife. Anne Mellor points out that, although Godwin "continued to demand that Shelley give him money, he refused to see or write Mary for . . . three-and-a-half years" (Mellor, 22). It seems that Godwin never doubted the justice of accepting Shelley's financial support since—in a burst of enthusiasm for his recently discovered mentor—Shelley had promised to contribute to Godwin in 1817. Godwin's financial arrangement with Shelley did not alter his vehement disapproval of Shelley's and Mary's elopement, however. Insofar as Victor Frankenstein rejects his monstrous child's unbridled affections, then, he may be modeled on William Godwin, and the parallel between *Frankenstein* and Mary Shelley's life may further clarify the novel.

Chapter 13, the third episode of the Creature's autobiography, begins with the Creature's promise to "relate events that impressed me with feelings which, from what I had been, have made me what I am" (158). In other words, we are to learn why he changes from a gentle creature who "could not conceive how one man could go forth to murder his fellow, or even why there were laws and governments" (161), to one who, having murdered a child and cunningly implicated an innocent young woman in his crime, demands a mate as "deformed and horrible" as himself (185).

According to the Creature, the first significant event leading to his transformation from philanthropist to criminal misanthrope was the entry of a lady "of angelic beauty" into the De Lacey family circle. It seems odd that the appearance of Felix's long-lost love, Safie, should be the first in a series of incidents leading to the Creature's degradation. But when the nature and degree of Safie's influence in the family are carefully considered, it becomes clear that her presence yields as much discontent as pleasure in the Creature. Previously, he had witnessed rather tame, thoughtful interchanges between the family members, who were as frequently sorrowful as happy. Now, however, he sees that Safie's "presence diffused gladness through the cottage, dispelling their sorrow as the sun dissipates the morning mists. Felix seemed peculiarly happy" (159). The possibility of such "peculiar" happiness had been previously unknown to the Creature, even through his vicarious experiences with the De Laceys. Learning that a vivacious young woman can bring such intense and universal joy to a despondent family is the first insight that arouses the Creature's desire for a mate of his own. The frustration of that precise desire in the Creature finally brings about the destruction of Victor Frankenstein's world.

Safie not only becomes the center of attention and affection for the De Lacey family and the Creature but also serves as a catalyst for the Creature's education. In thus becoming the surrogate object of his desire and also the means of his attaining knowledge, then, Safie becomes both "dissatisfying" and doubly enticing. For the Creature finds education a mixed blessing: "But sorrow only increased with knowledge. . . . Of what a strange nature is knowledge! It clings to the mind, when it has once seized on it, like a lichen on the rock. I wished sometimes to shake off all thought and feeling" (162). As Felix tutors Safie in the De Laceys' language through works of history, philosophy, and literature, so the Creature learns to speak and think like a human. He picks up such perennial biases of Western culture as "the slothful

Asiatics . . . the stupendous genius . . . of the Grecians . . . and wonderful virtue of the early Romans" (161). Having observed earlier that "the young man was constantly employed out of doors, and the girl in various labors within" (152), he now absorbs notions about "the difference of sexes, and the birth and growth of children; how the father doated on the smiles of the infant, and the lively sallies of the older child; how all the life and cares of the mother were wrapped up in the precious charge; how the mind of youth expanded and gained knowledge; of brother, sister, and all the various relationships which bind one human being to another in mutual bonds" (162). Edified by what he learns of human bonding, the Creature becomes progressively more unhappy with his own condition. Implicit in the Creature's lessons, however, is the flawed logic that makes the social system he mentally masters unworkable for him. In a scheme where interdependent beings fall into well-defined categories—father, mother, brother, sister—there is no place for one who does not fit in. Nor is there the possibility for true equality or absolute freedom.

The inflexibility of the system of human society that the Creature so desperately desires to enter extends even to appearances, as he will soon be reminded. His size and unconventional looks make him abhorrent, a freak. It is his prior condition as the illegitimate product of "unhallowed arts," however, that makes him impossible to categorize and therefore impossible to love. A conundrum of modern Western civilization—one especially meaningful to a talented young woman like Mary Shelley—is thus personified in the Creature: how can one maintain one's individuality and still fit in?

Viewing the world from his most separate of all spheres, the Creature draws conclusions about his own needs and rights first from close observations of the De Lacey family and later from his reading. With the insights he has gained from both observing Safie's influence on the family and absorbing the lessons Felix teaches her, the Creature is able to continue his education independently. The biases he has assimilated along with his early observations and lessons, however, color all his remaining education and behavior. Having studied *Paradise Lost,* for example, the Creature imaginatively conflates Safie with Milton's Eve (the *original* feminine dissatisfier). Observing the increasing happiness of the De Laceys after Safie's arrival, the Creature experiences feelings that become "every day more tumultuous [sometimes allowing] my thoughts, unchecked by reason, to ramble in the fields of Paradise, and dar[ing] to fancy amiable and lovely creatures sympathizing with my feelings and cheering my gloom; their angelic countenances breathed smiles of consolation. But it was all a dream; no Eve soothed my sorrows nor shared my thoughts" (172). The coincidence of the Creature finding a copy of *Paradise Lost* (1674) and using it as a sort of history or behavioral guide is not as unlikely as it might seem. Milton's epic of fallen man was a particular favorite among the romantics (as was Goethe's *Sorrows of Young Werther* [1774], another of the Creature's "finds"). For the most part Mary Shelley's contemporaries interpreted *Paradise Lost* as a justification of *man*'s or Satan's ways to men rather than as a means to "justifie the wayes of God to men," as Milton intended. The identification implied in the Creature's reveries of Milton's Eve with Safie reinforces the contradictory nature of Safie's role both in the novel and in Mary Shelley's imagination. The Creature's ideal woman, like Mary Shelley's, was colored by a depiction of Eve as a contingent being, a helpmate and afterthought who exists only to complement man. In thinking for herself, Eve oversteps her bounds, as does Safie. But Safie goes only as far as Western culture will allow. She escapes the confinement of the harem for the freedom of Felix's family, another realm legally dominated by men.

The Creature's unfulfilled desire for his Safie-inspired Eve combines with his thirst for revenge to produce one of the richest and most enigmatic scenes in the novel. As he bends over the sleeping Justine, who, like Safie, is "one of those whose joy-imparting smiles are bestowed on all but [him]" (184), he whispers, "Awake, fairest, thy lover is near—he who would give his life but to obtain one look of affection from thine eyes; my beloved, awake" (184). But no sooner has he uttered these phrases from a highly conventionalized Beauty and the Beast tradition than he makes an immediate about-face and, anticipating her horror and censure, determines to punish this innocent young woman for the murder *he* has committed. Why? "[Because I feel] forever robbed of all that she could give me, she shall atone. The crime had its source in her; be hers the punishment! Thanks to the lessons of Felix and the sanguinary laws of man, I had learned how to work mischief" (184). It is difficult to follow the Creature's logic here, perhaps because he is thinking not rationally but metaphorically, as Adam does in *Paradise Lost*. To find the source of his crime in this young girl is both insensitive and unreasonable. How can we account for the complete collapse of the monster's rationality and compassion? His anger and frustration are certainly understandable. Even the murder of William, who is related to Victor Frankenstein, may be explainable and in any case may have been accidental. But implicating an innocent, sleeping beauty who is entirely unknown to him is excessive. The passage was added for the 1831 edition of the novel, and more than any other single section, I believe, indicates Mary Shelley's confused position in the growing controversy about proper roles for women.

A possible solution to the puzzle of the Creature's abusive treatment of Justine is to imagine him as one facet of Mary Shelley's psychological state, and Justine—who belongs in the company of Margaret Saville, Caroline Beaufort Frankenstein, Elizabeth, Safie, Eve, and all idealized women—as a contending facet. The scene where the Creature sets up Justine by planting Caroline's miniature in her pocket then becomes the site of Mary Shelley's own psychological struggle with contending versions of herself. It is especially intriguing to consider that it is the Creature aspect of Mary Shelley that survives in the novel, albeit unhappy, alone, and preparing to die.

In this scene of psychological contention, the Creature's anger stems from a confused desire both to have and to be an unrealistically perfect mate. With uncanny foresight, the Creature arranges to place this false, impossible ideal of womanhood embodied in Justine on trial. He will later entirely eliminate another ideal of femininity, Elizabeth, the too-perfect bride of Frankenstein. In place of such false ideals, the Creature demands "a creature of another sex, but as hideous as myself. . . . We shall be monsters, cut off from all the world; but on that account we shall be more attached to one another. Our lives will not be happy, but they will be harmless and free from the misery I now feel" (187). Through the Creature, then, Mary Shelley seems symbolically to destroy a standard of feminine behavior and physical perfection that she may have consciously wished to fulfill, but that neither she nor any human woman could actually achieve. Also, through the practical demands of the Creature for an equal partner, she replaces a thoroughly false ideal with a somewhat flawed model that would nonetheless be given the same respect and chance for happiness as her mate. Notably, the Creature and his mate would not operate in separate spheres but would be "attached" to and dependent upon one another.

Later the Creature repeats his wish to "live in communion with an equal" (188), but his desire for true equality with a single mate will be thwarted even more dramatically than his wish for consolation from "lovely creatures" with "angelic countenances" (172) had been. Furthermore, both the Creature and his creator will remain "unbrided."

8

"The Marriage of Heaven and Hell"

"I will be with you on your wedding night!" Such was my sentence,
and on that night would the daemon employ every art to destroy me.
                                    —Victor Frankenstein to Robert Walton (228)

Most readers are amazed at Victor Frankenstein's naïveté in failing to
interpret the Creature's words, "I shall be with you on your wedding
night" (209), as a threat to Elizabeth rather than to himself. All the
Creature's past crimes point to the likelihood that he will revenge himself by destroying Victor's loved ones while saving his creator's life in
the hope of eventually acquiring a mate. Yet, recalling the Creature's
threat six times prior to his wedding, Victor foolishly persists in his
belief that the Creature intends to kill *him*. While Victor's incredible
obtuseness is one of many discrepancies we could cite as evidence of a
certain literary ineptness on Mary Shelley's part, the Creature's threat
and Victor's misreading of it are too obviously emphasized to have
been carelessly repeated. We must believe, then, that Mary Shelley
meant us to notice and question this glaring communication gap
between the Creature, his nemesis, and Elizabeth. The question is, why
does Victor misinterpret the threat?

On one level Victor's misinterpretation is meant to highlight his egocentricity. From earliest childhood he had been taught by the example of his parents to expect "inexhaustible stores of affection" from his family and friends. Even Elizabeth had been acquired as "a pretty present for . . . Victor" (79, 80). Thus Victor might feel that even the attention implied in the Creature's warning rightfully belongs to him.

Perhaps, too, Victor's strange behavior regarding the Creature's expressed intention of making himself an unwelcome wedding guest is meant to emphasize Victor's guilt, his Ancient Mariner–like sin against the community. At the very least, to save his family and neighborhood from further destruction, he should have come forward and taken responsibility for the Creature's crimes. At best he might have loved his creature as a son. But certainly he ought to have told Elizabeth his horrible secret *before* the wedding rather than immediately after, as he had promised. In addition to these facile explanations for Victor's inertia and its consequences, however, there is the possibility that Mary Shelley used the threat to highlight Elizabeth's shortcomings.

Elizabeth's failure to demand an explanation from Victor for his various absences and his antisocial behavior demonstrates her stereotypically feminine patience and good temper. Even when, in a letter, she does question Victor's intentions, her inquiry is almost painfully genteel and self-effacing: "Tell me, dearest Victor. Answer me, I conjure you, by our mutual happiness . . . Do you not love another? . . . when I saw you last autumn so unhappy, flying to solitude from the society of every creature, I could not help supposing that you might regret our connexion. . . . I who have so *disinterested* an affection for you, may increase your miseries tenfold by being an obstacle to your wishes" (228; emphasis mine). We might excuse Elizabeth's delicacy on the grounds that she really does love Victor so altruistically as to wish his happiness above all else. On the other hand, we might suppose that she has succumbed to certain cultural pressures, as Justine had done earlier by becoming properly "disinterested" in her own fate, free of desire and self-interest to such a degree that she lacks healthy passions. This hyperbolic goodness might be a calculated overstatement that Mary Shelley uses to force our judgment of Elizabeth's excessively sentimental tolerance. Possibly we are meant *not* to excuse her. Perhaps Mary Shelley, like the poet-artist William Blake in "The Marriage of Heaven and Hell" (1790), is reversing conventional definitions of good and evil when she employs her Creature to "murder" Elizabeth, "execute" Justine, and "hound" Victor Frankenstein to death. And maybe Elizabeth must share responsibility with Victor and his Creature for her own death.

William Blake, a friend of Mary Wollstonecraft and William Godwin, had been more radical than either in his notions of moral behavior. Likewise, the style and subject matter of his literature and art were more genuinely revolutionary than those of his romantic descendants Percy Shelley and Lord Byron. Again and again Blake insisted that typically good behavior—conduct restricted by rules of morality, custom, or reason—is actually evil, and typically evil behavior—unrestrained physical energy—is good:

> Energy is the only life and is from the body, and reason is the bound or outward circumference of energy. Energy is eternal delight.
> Those who restrain desire do so because theirs is weak enough to be restrained; and the restrainer or reason usurps its place and governs the unwilling.
> And being restrained it by degrees becomes passive, till it is only the shadow of desire.[1]

Mary Shelley had read Blake's works, and some critics believe that both "The Book of Urizen" (1794) and "The Marriage of Heaven and Hell" influenced her thinking. There is certainly need for more study of this relationship. While this is not the place for a full-blown examination of Blake's influence on *Frankenstein,* his eccentric ideas invite comparison with *Frankenstein*'s premises because they exemplify a cultural revulsion, if you will, away from "proper" behavior. Sharing some of Blake's disgust, especially for conventional middle-class "feminine" behavior, Mary Shelley seems to punish many of her female characters for adhering too closely to a model of propriety.

The evidence in *Frankenstein* reveals that although Mary Shelley's sympathy with Blake's ideas was only partial and somewhat tentative, it was real. Her critique of the heavenly behavior of women and (sometimes) hellish enterprises of men would have been reinforced by other voices in the culture as well. As we have seen in previous chapters, the pervasive revolutionary spirit that was operating in the early nineteenth century affected attitudes toward all conventional institutions, including marriage. "The Marriage of Heaven and Hell," although not *about* marriage in any ordinary sense, nonetheless reveals in its title and argument the persistent antagonism inherent in customary marital roles as they were perceived by the English middle classes. Blake's work concerns the tendency of customs, traditions, laws, and religious institutions to distort the truth about energy and desire. As such, it serves nicely to clarify several issues in *Frankenstein* centering on the monster's warning, Victor's misreading of it, and Elizabeth's murder.

Considered in the light of Blake's philosophy, the union of Elizabeth and Victor—the passive, accommodating angelic female, and the restless, passionate, "explosive" male—is not merely an example of a mismatch. It is a symbolic event heightened by its history of postponement, its ominously haunting threat, and its disastrous outcome. It portends the end of marriage as an institution as it was perceived in the nineteenth century. Given the marital role assignments current in Mary Shelley's world, one partner would always destroy the other. Mary Shelley herself, influenced by all sides of the debate about marriage, presents a complex image in which "proper" roles are never finally established. For, even as the self-effacing female seems to be temporarily idealized, and the egocentric male condemned, they are both destroyed in the long run.

In the preceding chapter I discussed the possibility that Justine is condemned because she represents an unattainable ideal of feminine behavior. Elizabeth's description of her makes it clear that Justine fits the pattern set for all *Frankenstein* women by Caroline Beaufort: "She is very clever and gentle and extremely pretty . . . her mien and her expression continually remind me of my dear aunt" (110). Her behavior during her imprisonment and trial intensifies the pattern, making that behavior both seductive and alarming. Prior to the trial, "the appearance of Justine was calm. She was dressed in mourning, and her countenance, always engaging, was rendered by the solemnity of her feelings, exquisitely beautiful" (124). Although during the trial itself, "her countenance had altered. Surprize, horror, and misery were strongly expressed" (125). Her subsequent responses are entirely unnatural, that is, they contradict the natural instinct for self-preservation.

We soon learn that Justine has falsely confessed her guilt under pressure from her confessor: "He threatened and menaced, until I almost began to think that I was the monster that he said I was. He threatened excommunication and hell fire in my last moments if I continued obdurate" (129). Finally, after Elizabeth makes the impossible promise to prove Justine's innocence in spite of the confession, Justine leaves Elizabeth with a challenge: "Learn from me, dear lady, to submit to the will of heaven" (130). The next day "the saintly sufferer" dies (131). Justine's mandate for Elizabeth to behave like a saint and martyr was added for the 1831 edition of *Frankenstein* during the period when, as we have seen, the woman's role as angel in the home was being loudly debated. Not only is this addition to the original text of *Frankenstein* important for assessing Justine's role, but it also reinforces an image of Elizabeth as, in effect, guaranteed to die as well.

In an earlier passage, also added for the 1831 edition, we learn that "the saintly soul of Elizabeth shone like a shrine-dedicated lamp" in the Frankensteins' peaceful home. Furthermore, Victor might have become "sullen in [his] study, rough through the ardour of [his] nature, but that [recalling Margaret Saville's care for Robert Walton] she was there to subdue [him] to a semblance of her own gentleness" (82–83). Numerous other references to Elizabeth's nature reinforce our sense of her heavenly qualities, her role as restrained restrainer of natural passion.

After Elizabeth's fatally ill adoptive mother, Caroline Beaufort Frankenstein, reveals her wish that Victor and Elizabeth will someday marry, Caroline resigns herself "cheerfully to death," while Elizabeth, veiling her grief, strives to act "the comforter to us all" (87, 88). Later, when she learns of William's death, she immediately assumes, in imagination, all the guilt and responsibility that Justine will later take on in reality: "Oh, God! I have murdered my darling child!" (116). When Justine is finally convicted and executed for William's murder, Elizabeth responds more naturally than she will ever do again in her short life. She becomes "sad and desponding; she no longer took delight in her ordinary occupations . . . eternal woe and tears she then thought was the just tribute she should pay to innocence so blasted and destroyed. . . . The first of these sorrows which are sent to wean us from the earth had visited her, and its dimming influence quenched her dearest smiles" (134). Like the children of Blake's *Songs of Innocence* (1789) and *Songs of Experience* (1794), and like the Creature, Elizabeth has temporarily lost her innocent vision of a civilized, orderly world and entered a lower world of experience where "men appear to [her] as monsters thirsting for each other's blood" (134). The irony is that her vision of a world inhabited by bloodthirsty men is more true than the prettified life she leads at home. The most important man in her life does indeed lust after blood. If anything, her disenchantment with "the world and its works" (134) should arouse her indignation to such passion that she would devote her life to preventing travesties like Justine's martyrdom. Instead, she quickly recovers her composure and takes up her role as ministering angel to Victor, whom she perceives as being more wretched than she: "Dear Victor, banish these dark passions. Remember the friends around you, who centre all their hopes in you. Have we lost the power of rendering you happy? Ah! While we love, while we are true to each other, here in this land of peace and beauty, your native country, we may reap every tranquil blessing—what can disturb our peace?" (135). These lines (which seem to anticipate the melancholy desperation of Matthew Arnold's poem "Dover Beach" [1867]) reveal the tragic flaw in Elizabeth's character. She is too ready to deny dark passions, too anxious to limit herself and others to the false security of their "native country." Elizabeth's vexed kinship with Margaret Walton Saville is evident here. As a servant of a civilized, tranquil society, she operates in ignorance of her man's separate sphere of activities.

Meanwhile, "encompassed by a cloud which no beneficial influence could penetrate" (135), Victor continues in his state of agitated despair until two months after Justine's death. Then, amid the sublime and consoling heights of the Alps, he meets his Creature and reluctantly listens to his story. At its conclusion, the Creature makes a demand that goes unfulfilled and therefore leads to two utterly failed marriages. In a sense, these failures constitute the tragedy of the novel.

After Alphonse Frankenstein asks whether Victor would object to "an immediate solemnization" of his marriage to Elizabeth, there occurs a passage in which the language creates a marriage "knot" that admits no solution. Revolving "a multitude of thoughts" in his mind, Victor attempts to come up with an answer for his father:

> Alas! To me the idea of an immediate union with my Elizabeth was one of horror and dismay. I was bound by a solemn promise which I had not yet fulfilled and dared not break, or if I did, what manifold miseries might not impend over me and my devoted family! Could I enter into a festival with this deadly weight yet hanging round my neck and bowing me to the ground? I must perform my engagement and let the monster depart with his mate before I allowed myself to enjoy the delight of a union from which I expected peace. (193)

Victor's kinship with the Ancient Mariner, and our kinship, as readers, with Victor, his family, *and* the Creature, are particularly significant in this passage. The "deadly weight" hanging around Victor's neck, by which he seems to mean the promise to the Creature, compares to the Mariner's Albatross, symbol of man's communion with all of nature. The "festival" is the marriage feast. We become potential wedding guests along with Robert Walton and his sister Margaret, through whom we are hearing the story. But the language of the passage makes the message more ambiguous than the allusion to Coleridge's poem suggests. Victor's declaration that the idea of immediate union with Elizabeth fills him with "horror and dismay," his later reference to "a solemn promise," and his affirmation that "I must perform my engagement," make it difficult to say what his feelings about marriage with Elizabeth really are. It is impossible to decide whether his engagement to Elizabeth or his promise to create a female monster fills him with more dread.

The immediate solution to Victor's dilemma is postponement of his wedding for as much as a year. Elizabeth readily agrees with this delay, apparently on the understanding that they will be wed "immediately on [Victor's] return" (194). But she seems to require no information about Victor's occupations during this time and, cooperating with Victor's father, arranges for Henry Clerval rather than herself to accompany her fiancé. The undisclosed purpose of Victor's absence is, of course, to create a mate for the monster. But, as we learn, Victor fails to complete the female Creature; in fact, "trembling with passion, [he] tore to pieces the thing" he had begun (207). Ironically, it seems not to occur to Victor that the monster may revenge his lost bride-to-have-been by similarly violating Victor's intended. Victor's rationale for destroying the monster's bride is telling: "She, who in all probability was to become a thinking and reasoning animal, might refuse to comply with a compact made before her creation. They might even hate each other [or, alternatively] a race of devils might be propagated upon the earth who might make the very existence of the species of man a condition precarious and full of terror" (206). To be precise, Victor is afraid that the female monster will be the equal of her mate (who had requested just such a companion). Unlike Elizabeth, and even the more liberated Safie, she might assert her right to break a contract made without her specific consent. In effect, she might enter the camp of those real-life "monstrous" women in the nineteenth century who were demanding equal status before the law. Or, the monsters might increase and multiply, thereby producing offspring who would challenge the institutions of man. Later we learn that Victor resolved to destroy the female Creature after having convinced himself that fulfilling his promise would have been "an act of the basest and most atrocious selfishness, and [he] banished . . . every thought that could lead to a different conclusion" (211).

Thus closing his mind to the Creature's point of view, Victor is directly responsible for the destruction of a potentially powerful, assertive woman—the female Creature—as he had been indirectly responsible for the demise of the ideal passive woman embodied in Justine. His behavior suggests that he fears both female images, and his handling of the Creature's threat establishes his guilt conclusively. By destroying one and exposing another woman to death, he successfully circumvents marriage for his Creature and for himself. Rather than immediately informing Elizabeth of the danger he must know her to be in, he thinks of "her tears and endless sorrow, when she should find her lover so barbarously snatched from her" (209). Clearly it is himself, not Elizabeth, for whom he grieves.

Even after Henry Clerval falls to the Creature's wrath, Victor neither confesses his duplicity in the murder nor warns Elizabeth of her imminent danger. Rather, he briefly considers whether he should declare himself "guilty and suffer the penalty of the law, less innocent than poor Justine had been" (219). The reader might well ask how Victor could be less innocent than Justine, who, we know, did not murder William. But Justine was not entirely innocent. In assuming the role of saint and martyr, Justine had conspired in her execution. Similarly, through her silence, Elizabeth tacitly agrees to her own murder. It is during Victor's recovery from the shock of Clerval's murder that Elizabeth writes to assure him of her "disinterested affection" (228). The letter is ambiguous enough to suggest that Elizabeth herself wishes to break off the engagement but is too self-effacing, and perhaps too unsure of her future, to do so. Nonetheless, she leaves Victor with the belief that she wishes the engagement to be fulfilled. Upon reading the letter, Victor is reminded of the Creature's warning and thinks, "If the monster executed his threat, death was inevitable; yet, again, I considered whether my marriage would hasten my fate" (228). The ambiguous juxtaposition of "threat," "death," and "marriage" reinforces the already well established relationships between these concepts in the novel. But if the connection is not made strong enough in this passage, Victor's direct response to Elizabeth significantly intensifies the shared responsibility of Victor, Elizabeth, and the Creature for the wedding night murder:

> Chase away your idle fears; to you alone do I consecrate my life and my endeavours for contentment. I have one secret Elizabeth, a dreadful one; when revealed to you, it will chill your frame with horror, and then, far from being surprised at my misery, you will only wonder that I survive what I have endured. I will conclude

this tale of misery and terror to you the day after our marriage
shall take place, for, my sweet cousin, there must be perfect confidence between us. But until then, I conjure you, do not mention
or allude to it. . . . I know you will comply. (229)

Unfortunately, Victor knows his fiancée too well; she perfectly
acts her part by complying with his request never to ask about his horrible secret. In spite of this letter's extraordinary contradictions, which
almost demand to be immediately questioned, Elizabeth welcomes
Victor with "gentleness and soft looks" (229). She seems to accept his
admonition to "chase away [her] idle fears" while ignoring his references to imminent "horror," "misery," and "terror." In many ways the
letter seems to be a challenge—Victor's unconscious way of asking
Elizabeth to call him to account for his sins and save them both.

However, even Victor's subsequent fits of madness do not rouse
Elizabeth to protect herself, nor do they inspire her to seek his confession. Instead, "she would remonstrate and endeavour to inspire me
with resignation." Victor's father, also choosing to ignore the ominous
implications of his son's erratic behavior, urges Victor's "immediate
marriage with Elizabeth" (230). To his credit, Victor momentarily
"remained silent," allowing his father to take his hesitation as a clue
about his ambiguous frame of mind. But when his father asks if Victor
has some other attachment standing in the way of his union with
Elizabeth, Victor passes up the opportunity to confess and deceptively
declares, "I love Elizabeth and look forward to our union with delight.
Let the day therefore be fixed; and on it I will consecrate myself, in life
or death, to the happiness of my cousin" (230).

Victor then recalls the Creature's threat yet again; but regarding
his *own* fate as unavoidable, he nonetheless agrees with his father
(apparently without consulting Elizabeth) that the "ceremony should
take place in ten days." Thinking ahead to the actual consequences of
his choice, he asserts that he would rather have banished himself and
"wandered a friendless outcast over the earth than have consented to
this miserable marriage" (230). In other words, he would have traded
places with the Creature. But claiming that the Creature has mysteri-
ously clouded his mind, he unwittingly hastens Elizabeth's death.

We learn, though, that in spite of her well-rehearsed role as passive angel, even Elizabeth develops suspicions about the danger her marriage represents. Victor's forced hilarity "hardly deceived the ever-watchful and nicer eye of Elizabeth. She looked forward to [their] union with placid contentment, not unmingled with a little fear, which past misfortunes had impressed, that what now appeared certain and tangible happiness might soon dissipate into an airy dream and leave no trace but deep and everlasting regret" (231). Elizabeth's "placid contentment" overcomes her "little fear" to such an extent that she seems unnaturally calm for a bride-to-be. Saintly as she is, Elizabeth is unable to entirely suppress her misgivings. On her wedding day "she was melancholy, and a presentiment of evil pervaded her; and perhaps she thought of the dreadful secret which [Victor] had promised to reveal to her on the following day" (231–32). Nevertheless, she does not postpone the ceremony, nor does she confront Victor with her fears and suspicions.

After the ceremony, under pressure from Victor to let him "taste the quiet freedom from despair that this one day permits" (232), she reverts to type and becomes his comforter and diversion. Her mood continues to fluctuate between joy and distraction, however, and only with difficulty is she able to maintain her decorum. Finally, when Victor—pistol in hand—becomes as agitated as the violent storm that has blown up around them, the terrified Elizabeth asks, "What is it that agitates you my dear Victor? What is it you fear?" Instead of answering her straightforward question candidly, Victor hushes her and declares, "This night is dreadful, very dreadful" (234).

Surely one whose self-preservation instinct was intact would pursue her line of questioning further. Instead, Elizabeth not only complies with Victor's remonstrances to interrogate him no further, she agrees to "retire" alone to their bridal suite while he inexplicably paces about the passages of the house toting a gun and peering into corners. Soon enough, the "shrill and dreadful" scream that comes as a surprise to no one but Victor is heard. Hearing it, "the whole truth" overcomes him; when the scream is repeated, he rushes in to find what is, in effect, the classic Gothic death scene for a female victim: "the purest creature of earth . . . lifeless and inanimate, thrown across the bed, her

71

head hanging down and her pale and distorted features half covered by her hair . . . her bloodless arms and relaxed form flung by the murderer on its bridal bier" (235). It would seem that the Creature has been as violent with Elizabeth as Victor had been with the Creature's mate.

It is thus, through an unconscious conspiracy between Victor, his Creature, and Elizabeth, that two "types" of women are eliminated, two marriages are prevented, and no one lives happily ever after. The implications for Mary Shelley and her culture seem to be that there can be no successful marriage that does not recognize in both partners elements of heaven and hell.

9

The Groomsmen

He is dead who called me into being; and when I shall be no more,
the very remembrance of us both will speedily vanish.
—The Creature to Robert Walton (260)

Throughout this reading of *Frankenstein* I have focused on the question of marriage, arguing that it is an important subject of the novel. Until recently, this emphasis would have seemed eccentric, and in fact it deviates from the norm of *Frankenstein* criticism. That norm, though somewhat amorphous, has traditionally centered on the relationship between Victor Frankenstein and his Creature. Even a modern critic can refer to the novel as "the story of Frankenstein and his monster" without expecting to be contradicted (Baldick, 1), for the urge to concentrate one's attention on the two obviously *main* characters is almost irresistible.

While this reading has not ignored Victor and his Creature or caused their "very remembrance [to] speedily vanish," as the chapter epigraph predicts, it has given prominence instead to minor characters, especially the women. But to leave the impression that favoring a feminine perspective is the only correct way of reading *Frankenstein* would be false. "Correct" approaches to *Frankenstein* are as numerous as the critical schools—psychological, historicist, mythological, and so on—that treat it, and as varied as the philosophical issues raised in the novel itself. A truly well informed reading of any complex work like *Frankenstein* would consider all approaches.

Although it is impossible to balance this particular study so that it equally provides, say, a romantic or a science fiction interpretation along with the biographical-historicist one I have attempted, it is possible to recount some of the recurring tenets in these two dominant critical assessments of Victor and his monster. Given two traditional views of the novel along with my modern one, the reader may then discover how interpretations deviate, converge, and become transformed by currents of thought in the text itself, the culture, and the reader's own increasingly sophisticated mind.

The earliest and most persistent treatment of the two antiheroes of *Frankenstein* involves a conflation of their characters, an intentional confusion of master and creature within the framework of the Prometheus myth. In Greek mythology Prometheus is a Titan who, in one version of the myth, creates the first men from potter's clay. In other versions, he steals fire from the gods to benefit humankind. In all versions, the gods punish him for his presumption by restraining him in chains. The full title of Mary Shelley's novel, *Frankenstein; or, The Modern Prometheus,* immediately predisposes the reader to interpret the work in the context of current Prometheus myth variants, like that of Goethe who—to oversimplify—saw the Titan as a rebel against the restrictions of society. The quotation from Milton's Adam in *Paradise Lost* just below the subtitle of *Frankenstein* complicates while reinforcing the novel's Promethean correspondence:

> Did I request thee, Maker, from my clay
> To mould me man?
> Did I solicit thee
> From darkness to promote me?—

This epigraph implies that the story is about a hapless creature as much as it is about an overreaching hero. Taken together, the two allusions imply a conflation of Greek and Judeo-Christian mythologies. References within the text itself also justify reading the novel as a modification of the Prometheus myth as well as an exploration of the creator-creature relationship. For example, when Victor refers to the Creature as "the living monument of presumption" (203), his early nineteenth-century audience, primed by numerous other treatments of the Titanic rebel, would have read "presumption" as an epithet for Prometheus. The Creature then becomes either the legacy of Prometheus (Victor) or Prometheus himself, and Victor stands for either Prometheus or one of the gods who restrained him in chains. The Creature's gift of firewood to his human family, the De Laceys, compares with Prometheus's gift of fire to humankind, but Victor's presumption in creating a new species of being establishes him even more firmly than the Creature in the Promethean camp.

A passage late in the novel makes the interchangeable natures of Victor and the Creature and the confusion of their Promethean roles more obvious. Just after Victor destroys the female Creature, the Creature warns, "I can make you so wretched that the light of day will be hateful to you. You are my creator, but I am your master; obey!" (208). Even the Creature's lament at the opening of this chapter implies an overlapping of his own identity with his maker's. Obvious clues like these have led critics to conclude that *Frankenstein* is one among many romantic reconstructions of Western mythology, one that plays off the Greek and Judeo-Christian world views (Prometheus and Adam being conflated) and incorporates a modern concern about the ways in which civilization is advancing.

This latter-day blend of the two most influential Western philosophies assesses what we might call the primary human conflict differently than does either its Greek or its Christian component. Rather than viewing the universal conflict as an interminable antagonism between the gods, humans, and their mediators, as the Greeks had done, or between God and Satan over the souls of humankind, as the Judeo-Christians do, the romantics saw the conflict as one between the individual and his or her own consciousness. Idealist philosophies like that of Immanuel Kant had done much to reinforce this concern. It is easy to understand how, given the emphasis on human ideas as the foundation and cause of human behavioral systems, a preoccupation with the "psychic split," which the romantics saw as endemic to human nature, would come about. However, the romantic critique of society did not stop at individual consciousness. Becoming increasingly complex, the romantic worldview often projected the fundamental human conflict as one between the individual consciousness and the social, psychological, and physical structures it had itself helped create and within which it had become trapped. Seen through these lenses (which, incidentally, work quite well even for modern readers), *Frankenstein* is "about" Victor's mishandling of his own suppressed desires or fantasies (imaginary constructs), to which he first gives form (as the Creature) and then later rejects. In this reading, Victor may be interpreted as an individual or as humankind's champion or representative. Perhaps the aspect of this romantic schema that is most difficult to accept is the lack of a facile way of determining the difference between good and evil. Judging by romantic tenets, it is not clear, for example, exactly what Victor's sin is: indulging his fantasy, or rejecting it? To complicate the matter, Victor's incarnated fantasy turns out, for many readers, to be more noble than he.

When critics have evaluated Victor in his own right and not as one half of a double-minded protagonist, he has typically been seen as a well-intentioned, brilliant scientist run amok. He may be guilty of Promethean ambition, but he is not necessarily evil. His great mistake is to isolate himself from humankind while purportedly creating a boon for that same humankind. In effect, he fails to balance "solitude" with "sympathy." These two words appear again and again in the novel and are meant to impress the reader with the necessity for both and the dangers of participating in an excess of either. Rousseau strongly influenced romantic notions about the need for solitude and self-reflection balanced with sympathy between individuals and between humankind and nature. Equally influential was Adam Smith's *The Theory of Moral Sentiments*. Published in 1759, the treatise argues that moral behavior is motivated by sympathy for others. According to

Smith, acting on our sympathetic feelings not only gives pleasure but moderates our natural egocentricity. Victor Frankenstein clearly exceeds the limits of healthy solitude and, in spite of frequent professions to the contrary, has no *active* sympathy for anyone but himself. He talks about his strong feelings for others but seldom takes action on their behalf.

Mary Shelley's depiction of Victor as a scientist obsessed with his research grew out of real concern about eighteenth- and early nineteenth-century advancements in chemistry, biology, and electrical engineering. For example, some critics believe that Victor Frankenstein's character may have been partly inspired by Mary Shelley's interest in the life of Sir Humphrey Davy, a professor of chemistry at the Royal Institution in London who enthusiastically anticipated a brave new world of perfect people realized through advances in chemistry. In any case, Victor's character fits the profile of the brilliant but eccentric, preoccupied scientist and has done more to ensure the permanence of that model in our cultural consciousness than any other fictional character.

The model Victor typifies features a scientist who begins with noble, humanitarian ideals but becomes so obsessed with his project that he loses sight of its possible negative consequences. A descendant of Victor Frankenstein who incorporates both the idea of the psychic split and the benevolent-scientist-turned-fanatic is Dr. Henry Jekyll, the altruistic side of the abhorrent Mr. Hyde. This scientist-demon model was a natural for the romantic imagination since it could readily be accommodated to the Promethean myth. Having stolen fire or light from the gods to give to man, Prometheus is the prototypical scientist as well as the champion of the imagination. Both "light" and "fire" may be interpreted symbolically *and* realistically to mean either inspiration or physical energy. Either way, Prometheus's gift, with its potential for destroying or enhancing existence, can be viewed as a curse as well as a blessing. Victor's right to the title of "the Modern Prometheus" is firmly established by his assertion that

> life and death appeared to me ideal bounds, which I should first break through, and pour a torrent of light into our dark world. A

new species would bless me as its creator and source; many happy and excellent natures would owe their being to me. No father could claim the gratitude of his child so completely as I should deserve theirs. Pursuing these reflections, I thought that if I could bestow animation upon lifeless matter, I might in process of time . . . renew life where death had apparently devoted the body to corruption. (98)

The Promethean and even Satanic lust for power that pervades this passage, in spite of its overt statement of concern about "our dark world" and bodily "corruption," locates Victor securely in the ranks of the criminally obsessed scientist. Assuming this reading of Victor's character, the Creature must be viewed as the product of Victor's scientific labor and judged an incarnation of energy indiscriminately released into an unsuspecting and unprepared world. The Creature thus becomes a threat to the very community whose lives he was meant to enhance. Like chemical waste or nuclear power that is not carefully channeled toward life-supporting ends, he haunts the community and his creator, demanding attention and threatening revenge.

Recently the scientific community in the United States has registered concern about the image of the irresponsible, obsessed scientist who is insensitive to human concerns and devoted either to abstract science for science's sake or to the advancement of industry and commerce. *Frankenstein* and its variants have actually been cited as being partially responsible for promulgating that image.[1] This response from the scientific community attests to the tenacious hold *Frankenstein* has on our collective imagination and justifies the novel's position as the archetypal work of science fiction.

No discussion of *Frankenstein*'s men would be complete without fully acknowledging the role Percy Shelley played in their formulation. Although some recent critics feel that his direct responsibility for the novel has been greatly exaggerated, there seems little doubt that he inspired certain aspects of Victor, Felix, Henry Clerval, and even the Creature. A consideration of Percy Shelley's influence will naturally take us back into the realm of biographical-historicist criticism where this study began. It should be clear by now, however, that the romantic and science fiction readings of *Frankenstein* briefly summarized above rely on a knowledge of the cultural context Mary Shelley inhabited almost as much as a biographical-historicist interpretation does.

We know by way of a 21 August 1816 entry in her journal that Mary Shelley talked about her "story" with Percy Shelley. We also know that he encouraged her to expand the story into a novel, that he helped correct the manuscript, and that he wrote a preface for it. Her permission, given in a letter written when he was away taking care of publishing problems, allowing him "carte blanche to make what alterations" he pleased has led some critics to view him as a co-author (or "ghostwriter," as I have suggested earlier). However, careful comparison of the text to both Mary's and Percy's writing styles, and extensive examination of notes, letters, and journals, has convinced recent scholars that Mary Shelley was indeed the real author of *Frankenstein* and that Percy Shelley was nothing more than her well-informed, responsible, and sympathetic editor (Sunstein, 124, 127, 131, 144, 392, 430–31, 433; Mellor, 57–68).

From my point of view, Percy Shelley's most important contribution to *Frankenstein* was the inspiration of his volatile and unusually complex personality. Mary Shelley may even have chosen "Victor" for her protagonist's name because as a young boy Percy had sensed the power that the name implied and assigned it to himself. Victor Frankenstein's interest in science, his tendency to become obsessively enthusiastic about whatever project he had currently under way, his need for periodic isolation, his powers of persuasion, his alternating fits of anguish and joy—all correspond with the facts of Percy Shelley's life. Even Victor's reluctance to marry, his use of laudanum, and the frequent contradictions between what he says and does match Percy Shelley's profile. Like Victor, Percy had been spoiled in early childhood by his mother and sisters, but his later unconventional beliefs and behavior estranged him from them. Percy Shelley was surely more balanced than Victor, however, and some critics see in Henry Clerval a more Shelleyan character.

Most likely, both characters were influenced by aspects of Percy Shelley. Clerval's willingness to take on "feminine" roles reflects Percy

Shelley's attitude—and indeed it was a general romantic belief—that men should become more feminized. To emphasize his feminine qualities, Clerval is often characterized in the same terms as Elizabeth. He is, for example, a "kind and attentive nurse" (105). He is also interested in literature rather than science, a characteristic considered by many in Mary Shelley's culture (and in our own) to be typically feminine. He is a humanitarian rather than an abstract philosopher. Percy Shelley, of course, was scientist, philosopher, and poet. Thus it seems likely that the characters of Victor and Clerval represent another sort of psychic split, one inspired by contending attitudes within the culture, attitudes that Percy Shelley himself found compatible with each other. Victor's remark "In Clerval I saw the image of my former self" (199) strengthens the argument for viewing the two as parts of a perfect whole. (I have discussed Percy Shelley's kinship with Felix De Lacey, another Clerval-like character, at some length in chapter 6.)

It is not surprising to find so many parallels between the men in *Frankenstein* and the most important man in Mary Shelley's life during its composition. Percy Shelley was not only her lover and husband but her friend and mentor. What's more, he was physically available for her to observe in all his moods during much of *Frankenstein*'s gestation period. We have seen, too, that William Godwin made a mark on the character of Victor Frankenstein in the judgmental-father model he provided. Safie's father may also owe something to William Godwin's example. The indirect impact of his novels, especially *Caleb Williams,* is apparent, too. Caleb is first pursuer and then quarry of his master, Falkland, and like Victor and the monster, the two eventually become psychologically interchangeable.

Still, Percy Shelley remains the most obvious model for *Frankenstein*'s men. Furthermore, he contributed significantly to the Creature's character. As a schoolboy, Percy Shelley, "meek-looking, delicate, narrow-chested, beardless, small-featured, long-haired, shrill-voiced," had undoubtedly felt out of place in the "all-male world of the English public school." His cousin, Thomas Medwin, is said to have remembered that Percy Shelley had been ridiculed for his "girlishness."[2] Later he was expelled from Oxford for publishing the pamphlet *The Necessity of Atheism* (1811) and was all but disowned by his family. Denounced by conservative politicians for championing the Irish cause and by moralists for his irregular sexual liaisons, he was considered by many among the middle classes to be psychologically if not physically deformed. Clearly, then, he knew rejection and must have occasionally felt, like the Creature, "spurned and deserted . . . [so that] a kind of insanity . . . burst all bounds of reason and reflection" (179).

Perhaps most notable of the Creature's similarities to Percy Shelley is his desire for an equal mate. By today's standards, Shelley's preferences in relationships between the sexes may seem too artificially chivalric on the one hand and too liberated on the other. But for its day, Shelley's philosophy was enlightened. Based partly on the eighteenth-century doctrine of sympathy, Shelley's philosophy for both sexes combined belief in a single standard of education, sexual freedom, and respect for sentiment and desire.

The Creature's demand for a female with whom he "can live in the interchange of those sympathies necessary" for his being (186), echoes Percy Shelley's philosophy. Even the Creature's preference for a mate as "hideous" as himself in a sense corresponds with Percy Shelley's attitude. For, in Shelley's estimation, the Creature's cultivation, sympathetic nature, and natural, animal-like agility (he "bounded over the crevices in the ice . . . with superhuman speed" [140]) would have rendered him beautiful. Presumably, his mate would have been equally endowed.

I have previously made the case that the Creature may have been inspired in part by Mary Shelley's own guilt. It may therefore seem farfetched to argue here that he also reflects certain aspects of Percy Shelley. But perhaps it is precisely because the Creature represents a nearly perfect balance of Mary and Percy Shelley at the most unspoiled and honest level of their beings that he has come to be viewed as the most interesting, believable, and complex character in the novel.

Mary Shelley calls the Creature her "hideous progeny," but in reality he is the product of a marriage of minds and sensibilities, those of Mary and Percy Shelley. Chapter 6 of this study emphasizes his sensitivity, a responsiveness to his own and others' feelings that runs the gamut from his wish for "gentle manners" (152) to his "tumultuous," indefinable desires (172) to "rage and revenge" (177). At times he might be Percy Shelley responding as a woman was expected to respond; at others he could be Mary Shelley reacting with typical "masculine" aggression. Even the Creature's education follows a pattern that Percy and Mary (and her parents before them) advocated. He is educated along with a "liberated" female, Safie, an arrangement that would have been unlikely in the real world of England. Furthermore, the very books the Creature and Safie learn from are the ones that Mary and Percy Shelley read together and discussed. Thanks to Felix, Safie's (and the Creature's) reading is eclectic; it includes works that cover all branches of knowledge and most of the known literary genres. The result of the Creature's co-education with a female by a male is a relatively balanced, extraordinarily *human* being. He is, of course, ruined by his enforced solitude and failure to meet arbitrary standards of physical beauty.

Yet he endures. After nearly all the beautiful people—the affected and self-deluded members of the Frankenstein family circle—have been destroyed, the Creature remains. In the end he is still the most honest and unpretentiously articulate character in the novel. Promising that his "spirit will sleep in peace" after his death (261), he is the Albatross rather than the Ancient Mariner speaking to us, the wedding guests. Seen in terms of the marriage conundrum considered throughout this study, you might say the Creature *is* a marriage—but too perfect a union of masculine and feminine qualities to be allowed into the mainstream of a civilization that still required that male and female operate in separate spheres.

Notes and References

Chapter 1

1. William St. Clair, *The Godwins and the Shelleys: The Biography of a Family* (New York: W. W. Norton, 1989), 219, hereafter cited in the text.

2. See Chris Baldick, *In Frankenstein's Shadow: Myth, Monstrosity, and Nineteenth-Century Writing* (Oxford: Clarendon, 1987), 16–18, hereafter cited in the text; and Warren Montag, " 'The Workshop of Filthy Creation': A Marxist Reading of *Frankenstein*," in *Frankenstein*, ed. Johanna M. Smith (New York: St. Martin's Press, 1992), 300–301.

3. See Paul O'Flinn, "Production and Reproduction: The Case of *"Frankenstein*," in *The Study of Popular Fiction: A Sourcebook*, ed. Bob Ashley (Philadelphia: University of Pennsylvania Press, 1989), 23–39.

Chapter 2

1. Terrence Holt, "Teaching *Frankenstein* as Science Fiction," in *Approaches to Teaching Shelley's "Frankenstein,"* ed. Stephen C. Behrendt (New York: Modern Language Association, 1990), 112–20. This is how Holt defines a work of science fiction in a class where he uses *Frankenstein* as both introduction to the course and "paradigm for the genre as a whole" (112).

Chapter 3

1. Review of *Frankenstein; or, The Modern Prometheus, Quarterly Review* 18 (January 1818): 379–85.

2. [Walter Scott], review of *Frankenstein; or, The Modern Prometheus, Blackwood's Edinburgh Magazine* NS2 (March 1818): 249–53; hereafter cited in text.

3. Anne K. Mellor, *Mary Shelley: Her Life, Her Fiction, Her Monsters* (New York: Methuen, 1988), 57–69, 219–24, hereafter cited in text.

4. Percy Bysshe Shelley, "On *Frankenstein*," in *The Works of Percy Bysshe Shelley in Verse and Prose*, ed. Harry Buxton Forman (London: Reeves and Turner, 1880), 7:11–14.

5. Quoted in Maurice Hindle's introduction to the Penguin Classics edition of *Frankenstein* (34).

6. Cited in Emily W. Sunstein, *Mary Shelley: Romance and Reality* (Boston: Little, Brown, 1989), 311, hereafter cited in text.

7. M. A. Goldberg, "Moral and Myth in Mrs. Shelley's *Frankenstein*," *Keats-Shelley Journal* 8, no. 1 (Winter 1959):27–38.

8. "*Frankenstein*," in *Masterplots: English Fiction Series*, ed. Frank N. Magill (New York: Salem Press, 1964), 235.

9. Harold Bloom, "*Frankenstein*; or, the New Prometheus," *Partisan Review* 32 (1965): 611–18.

10. Christopher Small, *Ariel Like a Harpy: Shelley, Mary, and Frankenstein* (London: Macmillan, 1954), reprinted as *Mary Shelley's Frankenstein: Tracing the Myth* (Pittsburgh: University of Pittsburgh Press, 1973); and L. J. Swingle, "Frankenstein's Monster and Its Romantic Relatives: Problems of Knowledge in English Romanticism," *Texas Studies in Literature and Language* 15 (1973): 51–65.

11. Ellen Moers, "Female Gothic," in *The Endurance of Frankenstein: Essays on Mary Shelley's Novel*, ed. George Levine and U. C. Knoepflmacher (Berkeley: University of California Press, 1979), 77–87.

12. Sandra M. Gilbert and Susan Gubar, *The Madwoman in the Attic: The Woman Writer and the Nineteenth-Century Imagination* (New Haven: Yale University Press, 1979), 213–47.

13. Barbara Johnson, "My Monster/My Self," *Diacritics* 12, no. 2 (Summer 1982): 2–10.

14. Mary Poovey, *The Proper Lady and the Woman Writer: Ideology as Style in the Works of Mary Wollstonecraft, Mary Shelley, and Jane Austen* (Chicago: University of Chicago Press, 1984), 114–42.

15. Gayatri Spivak, "Three Women's Texts and a Critique of Imperialism," in *"Race," Writing, and Difference*, ed. Henry Louis Gates, Jr. (Chicago: University of Chicago Press, 1986), 243–61.

16. William Veeder, *Mary Shelley and Frankenstein: The Fate of Androgyny* (Chicago: University of Chicago Press, 1986), hereafter cited in text.

17. William Walling, *Mary Shelley* (New York: Twayne, 1972); Jane Dunn, *Moon in Eclipse: A Life of Mary Shelley* (London: Weidenfeld & Nicolson, 1978); and Muriel Spark, *Child of Light: A Reassessment of Mary Wollstonecraft Shelley* (Hadleigh, England: Tower, 1951), revised and reprinted as *Mary Shelley: A Biography* (New York: Dutton, 1987).

18. Rosemary Jackson, "Narcissism and Beyond: A Psychoanalytic Reading of *Frankenstein* and Fantasies of the Double," in *Aspects of Fantasy,* ed. William Coyle (Westport: Greenwood Press, 1986); 45–53; and Judith A. Spector, "Science Fiction and the Sex War: A Womb of One's Own," *Literature and Psychology* 31 (1981): 21–32.

19. Samuel Holmes Vasbinder, "Scientific Attitudes in Mary Shelley's *Frankenstein*" (Ann Arbor: UMI, 1984); and Theodore Ziolkowski, "Science, Frankenstein, and Myth," *Sewanee Review* 89 (Winter 1981): 34–56.

20. Henriette Lazaridis Power, "The Text as Trap: The Problem of Difference in Mary Shelley's *Frankenstein*," *Nineteenth Century Contexts* 12, no. 1 (1988): 85–103.

21. Donald F. Glut, *The Frankenstein Catalog* (Jefferson, N.C.: McFarland & Co., 1984).

22. *The Ultimate Frankenstein,* ed. Byron Preiss (New York: Dell, 1991).

23. Stephen C. Behrendt, ed., *Approaches to Teaching Shelley's "Frankenstein"* (New York: Modern Language Association, 1990).

24. Johanna M. Smith, ed., *"Frankenstein": A Case Study in Contemporary Criticism* (New York: St. Martin's Press, 1992).

Chapter 4

1. Paula Feldman and Diana Scott-Kilvert, eds., *The Journals of Mary Wollstonecraft Shelley,* 2 vols. (Oxford: Clarendon, 1987), 560, hereafter cited in text as *Journals.*

2. Betty T. Bennett, ed., *The Letters of Mary Wollstonecraft Shelley,* 3 vols. (Baltimore: Johns Hopkins University Press, 1980–88), 1: 42.

3. See David Knight, *The Age of Science: The Scientific World-view in the Nineteenth Century* (Oxford: Basil Blackwell, 1986), especially chap. 3, "Wrestling with God."

Chapter 5

1. Quoted in Mary R. Beard, *Woman as a Force in History: A Study in Traditions and Realities* (New York: Octagon Books, 1976), 89.

2. Simone de Beauvoir, *The Second Sex* (New York: Vintage Books, 1974), 124–25.

3. Mary Wollstonecraft, *A Vindication of the Rights of Woman* (London J. M. Dent & Sons Ltd., 1929), 197.

4. Quoted in Susan Groag Bell and Karen M. Offen, eds., *Women, the Family, and Freedom: The Debate in Documents, vol. 1, 1750–1880.* (Stanford, Calif.: Stanford University Press, 1983), 182.

5. Quoted in Constance Rover, *Love, Morals, and the Feminists* (London: Routledge & Kegan Paul, 1970), 78, 94.

Chapter 8

1. William Blake, "The Marriage of Heaven and Hell," in *Blake: The Complete Poems,* 2d ed., ed. W. H. Stevenson (London: Longman House, 1989), 106.

Chapter 9

1. I was given this information by a colleague, Mary Hood, Professor of Biology at the University of West Florida, who heard the comments at an annual professional convention.

2. Nathaniel Brown, *Sexuality and Feminism in Shelley* (Cambridge, Mass.: Harvard University Press, 1979), 166.

Bibliography

Primary Works

Editions of *Frankenstein*

Frankenstein; or, The Modern Prometheus. 3 vols. London: Lackington, Hughes, Harding, Mayor & Jones, 1818.

Frankenstein; or, The Modern Prometheus. With an Introduction by "M.W.S." London: Henry Colburn and Richard Bentley; Edinburgh: Bell and Bradfute; Dublin: Cumming, 1831. A revised, one-volume edition.

Frankenstein; or, The Modern Prometheus: The 1818 Text. Edited by James Rieger. Chicago: University of Chicago Press, 1982.

Frankenstein; or, The Modern Prometheus. The Pennyroyal Press edition designed and illustrated by Barry Moser, with an afterword by Joyce Carol Oates. Berkeley and Los Angeles: University of California Press, 1984.

Frankenstein. Edited by Maurice Hindle. New York: Viking Penguin, 1985. Based on the 1831 text.

Frankenstein. Edited by Harold Bloom. New York: Signet-NAL, 1965. Based on the 1831 text.

The Annotated "Frankenstein." Edited by Leonard Wolf. New York: Potter, 1977. Based on the 1831 text.

"Frankenstein": A Case Study in Contemporary Criticism. Edited by Johanna M. Smith. New York: St. Martin's Press, 1992. Specifically aimed at college students and advanced high school students, this "Critical Casebook" edition includes the text of *Frankenstein,* a section on its

biographical and historical setting, and five analyses of the novel ranging in perspective from reader response to the new historicism. A most
effective introduction to current critical theory applied to the text of
Frankenstein.

Other Novels

Mathilda. Edited by Elizabeth Nitchie. Chapel Hill: University of North
Carolina Press, 1959.

Valperga: Or, The Life and Adventures of Castruccio, Prince of Lucca. 3 vols.
London: G. and W. B. Whittaker, 1823.

The Last Man. Edited by Hugh Luke, Jr. Lincoln: University of Nebraska
Press, 1965.

The Fortunes of Perkin Warbeck, A Romance. 3 vols. London: Henry Colburn
and Richard Bentley, 1830.

Lodore. 3 vols. London: Richard Bentley, 1835.

Falkner, A Novel. 3 vols. London: Saunders and Otley, 1837.

Other Works

Mary Shelley: Collected Tales and Stories. Edited by Charles E. Robinson.
Baltimore: Johns Hopkins University Press, 1976.

The Journals of Mary Wollstonecraft Shelley, 1814–1844. Edited by Paula
Feldman and Diana Scott-Kilvert. 2 vols. Oxford: Clarendon, 1987.

The Letters of Mary Wollstonecraft Shelley. Edited by Betty T. Bennett. 3 vols.
Baltimore: Johns Hopkins University Press, 1980–88.

Secondary Works

This list is limited to works dealing primarily with *Frankenstein* rather than
Mary Shelley's entire corpus of works, and to works that discuss Mary
Shelley's biographical relationship with *Frankenstein.*

Books

Baldick, Chris. *In Frankenstein's Shadow: Myth, Monstrosity, and Nineteenth-
Century Writing.* Oxford: Clarendon, 1987. Baldick discusses the transformations of the Frankenstein myth in the works of writers who came
after Mary Shelley as well as in the culture at large. A provocative reading that demonstrates how history and myth converge.

Bibliography

Behrendt, Stephen C., ed. *Approaches to Teaching Shelley's "Frankenstein."* New York: Modern Language Association, 1990. Though aimed at high school and college teachers, this collection of guides, articles, and bibliographies is exceptionally useful and readable for the student of *Frankenstein* as well.

Ketterer, David. *Frankenstein's Creation: The Book, The Monster, and Human Reality.* Victoria: University of British Columbia Press, 1979. Argues that the 1831 edition is preferable to the 1818 edition.

Levine, George, and U. C. Knoepflmacher, eds. *The Endurance of Frankenstein: Essays on Mary Shelley's Novel.* Berkeley: University of California Press, 1979. This collection of essays is one of the most often cited works on *Frankenstein*. It includes articles on the history and contexts of *Frankenstein* as well as biographical, feminist, and psychological interpretations. The section "The Visual Progeny: Drama and Film" establishes the precedent, now frequently followed, of discussing the novel in terms of its innumerable film distortions.

Mellor, Anne K. *Mary Shelley: Her Life, Her Fiction, Her Monsters.* New York: Methuen, 1988. An important feminist critique of Mary Shelley and her life and works in terms of her convictions about the centrality of the family to the ideal community. Includes important comparisons between the 1818 and 1831 texts.

Small, Christopher. *Ariel Like a Harpy: Shelley, Mary, and Frankenstein.* London: Macmillan, 1954. Reprinted as *Mary Shelley's Frankenstein: Tracing the Myth.* Pittsburgh: University of Pittsburgh Press, 1973. Discusses the influence of Percy Shelley on *Frankenstein,* currently a controversial issue.

Tropp, Martin. *Mary Shelley's Monster: The Story of Frankenstein.* Boston: Houghton Mifflin, 1976. The history of the Creature through various transformations. Includes a selected chronology of *Frankenstein* films.

Veeder, William. *Mary Shelley and Frankenstein: The Fate of Androgyny.* Chicago: University of Chicago Press, 1986. A "contextual" reading of *Frankenstein* that attempts, by placing the novel in the contexts of Mary Shelley's life, times, and other works, to show that she believed that an androgynous approach to life is necessary for the survival of humankind. Veeder believes that she despaired of seeing her vision attained, however. Insightful, useful work.

Critical Biographies

Bigland, Eileen. *Mary Shelley.* London: Cassell & Co., 1959.

Church, Richard. *Mary Shelley.* New York: Viking, 1928.

Dunn, Jane. *Moon in Eclipse: A Life of Mary Shelley.* London: Weidenfeld & Nicolson, 1978.

Gerson, Noel Bertram. *Daughter of Earth and Water: A Biography of Mary Wollstonecraft Shelley.* New York: William Morrow, 1973.

Grylls, R. Glynn. *Mary Shelley: A Biography.* London: Oxford University Press, 1938.

Harris, Janet. *The Woman Who Created Frankenstein: A Portrait of Mary Shelley.* New York: Harper & Row, 1975.

Leighton, Margaret. *Shelley's Mary: A Life of Mary Wollstonecraft Shelley.* New York: Farrar, Straus & Giroux, 1973.

Moore, Helen. *Mary Wollstonecraft Shelley.* Philadelphia: Lippincott, 1886.

Nitchie, Elizabeth. *Mary Shelley, Author of Frankenstein.* New Brunswick, N.J.: Rutgers University Press, 1953.

St. Clair, William. *The Godwins and the Shelleys: The Biography of a Family.* New York: W. W. Norton, 1989.

Spark, Muriel. *Child of Light: A Reassessment of Mary Wollstonecraft Shelley.* Hadleigh, Eng.: Tower, 1951. Revised and reprinted as *Mary Shelley: A Biography.* New York: Dutton, 1987.

Sunstein, Emily. *Mary Wollstonecraft Shelley: Romance and Reality.* Boston: Little, Brown, 1989.

Walling, William. *Mary Shelley.* New York: Twayne, 1972.

Articles and Parts of Books

Aldiss, Brian W. "The Origin of the Species, Mary Shelley." In *The Billion Year Spree: The True History of Science Fiction,* 1–39. Garden City, N.Y.: Doubleday, 1973.

Bloom, Harold. "*Frankenstein;* or, the New Prometheus." *Partisan Review* 32 (1965): 611–18.

Cude, Wilfred. "Mary Shelley's Modern Prometheus: A Study in the Ethics of Scientific Creativity." *Dalhousie Review* 52 (1972): 212–25.

Gilbert, Sandra M., and Susan Gubar. In *The Madwoman in the Attic: The Woman Writer and the Nineteenth-Century Literary Imagination,* 213–47. New Haven: Yale University Press, 1979.

Hirsch, Gordon D. "The Monster Was a Lady: On the Psychology of Mary Shelley's *Frankenstein.*" *Hartford Studies in Literature* 7 (1978): 116–53.

Kmetz, Gail. "Mary Shelley: In the Shadow of Frankenstein." *Ms.* (February 1975): 12–16.

Lund, Mary G. "Mary Godwin Shelley and the Monster." *University of Kansas City Review* 27 (1962): 253–58.

Millhauser, Milton. "The Noble Savage in Mary Shelley's *Frankenstein.*" *Notes and Queries* 190 (1946): 248–50.

Bibliography

Newman, Beth. "Narratives of Seduction and the Seductions of Narrative: The Frame Structure of *Frankenstein*." *ELH* 53 (1986): 141–63.

Oates, Joyce Carol. "Frankenstein's Fallen Angel." *Critical Inquiry* 10 (1984): 543–54.

O'Flinn, Paul. "Production and Reproduction: The Case of *Frankenstein*." In *Popular Fiction: Essays in Literature and History*, edited by Peter Humm, Paul Stigant, and Peter Widowson, 196–221. London: Methuen, 1986.

Pollin, Burton R. "Philosophical and Literary Sources of *Frankenstein*." *Comparative Literature* 17 (1965): 97–108.

Rieger, James. "Dr. Polidori and the Genesis of *Frankenstein*." *Studies in English Literature* 3 (1963): 461–72.

Rottensteiner, Franz. "The Modern Prometheus: Frankenstein, Mr. Hyde, and Dr. Moreau." In *The Science Fiction Book: An Illustrated History*, 32–35. New York: New American Library, 1975.

Spivak, Gayatri. "Three Women's Texts and a Critique of Imperialism." In *"Race," Writing, and Difference*, edited by Henry Louis Gates, Jr., 262–80. Chicago: University of Chicago Press, 1986.

Swingle, L. J. "Frankenstein's Monster and Its Romantic Relatives: Problems of Knowledge in English Romanticism." *Texas Studies in Literature and Language* 15 (1973): 51–66.

Bibliographies

Glut, Donald F. *The Frankenstein Catalog*. Jefferson, N.C.: McFarland & Co., 1984.

Ketterer, David. "Mary Shelley and Science Fiction: A Select Bibliography Selectively Annotated." *Science Fiction Studies* 5 (1978): 172–78.

Lyles, W. H. *Mary Shelley: An Annotated Bibliography*. New York: Garland, 1975.

Index

Index

Shelley, Harriet, 23
Shelley, Mary Wollstonecraft,
  10–12, 14, 55; birth of, 3;
  education of, 5; family of,
  22–23, 25, 26, 54 (*see also*
  Clairmont, Claire; Godwin,
  William; Wollstonecraft,
  Mary); literary influences on,
  5–6, 26, 63; and marriage, 22,
  23, 25–29, 32, 33, 42, 64; and
  Rousseau, 50

WORKS
  "Author's introduction" (of 1831
    revision of *Frankenstein*),
    26–29
  *Frankenstein; or, the Modern
    Prometheus*, 3, 8, 10, 24–25,
    74; cinematic variants of, 9,
    24, 28; Critical Casebook edi-
    tion of, 18; criticism of, 13–
    18, 73, 74; 1831 revision of,
    14, 17, 21, 22, 26–28, 36, 38,
    40, 65; marriage relationships
    in, 22, 23, 25–26, 31, 42,
    47–48; as modern myth, 12,
    75; as science fiction, 5–6, 9,
    11; and sexism, 5; and
    women's studies, 9, 11. *See
    also individual characters*
  History of a Six Weeks' Tour, 7
  *Journals of Mary Wollstonecraft
    Shelley, The, 1814–1844*, 42
Shelley, Percy, 4, 5–6, 8, 13, 25–26,
  27–28, 49; contributions to

Frankenstein of, 13, 14, 15,
  24, 25, 78–82; and marriage,
  23, 32; *The Necessity of
  Atheism*, 80; *Queen Mab*, 32
Small, Christopher: *Ariel Like a
  Harpy*, 16
Smith, Adam: *The Theory of Moral
  Sentiments*, 76–77
Spark, Muriel: *Child of Light*, 17
Spector, Judith A., 17
Spivak, Gayatri, 16
Swingle, L. J., 16

technology, 4, 7, 11. *See also* scientific advances

Ultimate Frankenstein, The, 18
utilitarianism, 8

Vasbinder, Samuel Holmes, 17
Veeder, William: *Mary Shelley and
  "Frankenstein,"* 16, 33
Villa Diodati, 15, 54

Walling, William: *Mary Shelley*, 17
Walton, Robert (character), 25, 30,
  31, 34, 36–40, 47
Wollstonecraft, Mary, 10–11, 22,
  49; and child rearing, 45;
  Juvenile Library of, 7; *A
  Vindication of the Rights of
  Woman*, 5, 35
women's rights, 3, 4

Ziolkowski, Theodore, 17

The Author

Mary Lowe-Evans, Associate Professor of English at the University of West Florida in Pensacola, was educated at Saint Mary's Dominican College in New Orleans, the University of Mississippi, and the University of Miami, which awarded her a Ph.D. degree in 1987. She has previously written one book, Crimes against Fecundity: Joyce and Population Control (1989), and over a dozen articles and reviews. Recently she has contributed to the Modern Language Association's volume Approaches to Teaching Joyce's Ulysses and to "Frankenstein": A Case Study in Contemporary Criticism. She lives with her husband, also an English professor, in Gulf Breeze, Florida. She has three children who have all, in one way or another, influenced her reading of Frankenstein.